ANCIENT EGYPT

ANCIENT EGYPT

Three Thousand Years of Splendor

By Warner A. Hutchinson

Grosset & Dunlap
A Filmways Company
Publishers New York

Produced and prepared by
Quarto Marketing, Ltd., New York

Designed by Ed Schneider

Editor: Anne Ziff
Production Coordinators:
Tammy O'Bradovich and Julianne Griffin

The author and publisher acknowledge with thanks all photographs
from ILLUSTRATED FAMILY ENCYCLOPEDIA OF THE
LIVING BIBLE Copyright © 1967 by San Francisco Productions,
Inc. Reproduced by permission of A. J. Holman, a division of J. B.
Lippincott Company.
Further acknowledgement and thanks to the Metropolitan Museum
of Art, Rogers Fund and Contribution from Edward S. Harkness,
1929, for the cover photograph of the Egyptian Sculpture Statue of
Queen Hatshepsut, detail, head frontal view.

The author expresses his special thanks to Ted Andrews
and Walter Ott, without whose help this book would
not have been possible.

To all my children:

Cynthia and Pamela,
Keryn and Wayne,
Ruth and Robert,
Sally, Bill, and Kevin.

Contents

EGYPT
Introduction

Close-ups of the remaining standing pillars in the temple of Amun at Karnak. These colossal pillars are 69 feet tall. They were built during the reigns of Seti I and Ramses II, a time in which Egyptian power abroad was beginning to decline. (13th century B.C.)

Napoleon Bonaparte gave ancient Egypt to the modern world. For centuries Egypt lay out of the mainstream, beyond world consciousness. Her timeless splendors had been known only to a few fearless adventurers who had dared to travel to that exotic place. They brought back strange tales of huge and wondrous temples and statues.

Napoleon invaded Egypt in 1798 to expand French influence against the British. He took hundreds of scholars with him. For over two years they studied the monuments of the past intensely. They drew superb pictures of everything they could find, from the Delta to the island of Elephantine. They took their findings back to Paris with them in 1801, when the British forced French withdrawal from Egypt.

During the next few decades their findings were published in luxuriously printed volumes. They captured the imagination of Europe. Ancient Egypt had been discovered!

The French had collected antiquities. Many of these were turned over to the British when Alexandria was surrendered. Transported to London, these relics of the pharaohs became the foundation of the British Museum's extensive Egyptian collection.

During the next hundred years, the ancient ruins were ravaged by entrepreneurs either to satisfy the whims of wealthy individual collectors or to feed the fierce competition between the world's major museums for Egyptian relics. The stunning collections in the Louvre, the Berlin Museum, the British Museum, the Metropolitan Museum of Art, and the Brooklyn Museum are founded on this early plunder of tombs and temples. The early exportation of antiquities was made possible by stealth or the bribery of Egyptian officials. The marvelous treasures of the Cairo Museum are either the leftovers from those early days or they are discoveries made since the time Egypt realized the importance of its own past and had the

will to enforce its laws prohibiting the exportation of antiquities without governmental approval.

Mysteries Unveiled

The mysteries of Egypt's history were unveiled once the heiroglyphic system of writing was understood. A brilliant French Egyptologist, Jean Francois Champollion, deciphered the famed Rosetta Stone on which the same message was repeated in three scripts: Greek, a cursive form of Egyptian writing, and hieroglyphics. This find was made early in the nineteenth century and gave great impetus to Egyptian studies.

Prior to the discovery of Tutankhamun's tomb in 1922, the most famous Egyptian relic was "Cleopatra's Needle." In fact, there were four elegant obelisks

Men often wore a short garment, fastened by a knot or by tucking the ends in at the waist. Wigs were common for both men and women. (Thebes, 15th century B.C.)

3

A noble is seen seated with his wife and his mother. Their fine furniture, beautiful garden, jewelry, hair styles, finely cut garments, and the delicacy of their eating and drinking indicate aristocratic refinement. Note the chair legs in the shape of the front and back legs of a lion. (Tomb of Userhet, 13th century B.C.)

known in the Western world by that name. None of them had anything to do with Queen Cleopatra.

Pharaoh Thutmose III erected four obelisks during the height of New Kingdom power, in which he commemorated his thirtieth anniversary as king. He wrote on them that his name would endure for all time. One obelisk was taken by Constantine to Constantinople, where it was eventually placed in the Hippodrome by Emperor Theodosius in 390 A.D. The second obelisk was taken to Rome and placed in the Circus Maximus in 363 A.D. It fell over and was buried for centuries. Pope Paul V recovered it and placed it in front of the papal palace of St. John Lateran in 1588. The third obelisk was presented to the British government in the late nine-

teenth century by the Egyptian pasha, who ruled the country as part of the Ottoman Empire. It was taken to London at the expense of a private citizen and placed on the Embankment alongside the Thames, not far from the Houses of Parliament. The fourth obelisk was given by Egypt to the United States in 1880. It stands in New York's Central Park just behind the Metropolitan Museum of Art. The regnal monuments of a king of imperial Egypt now stand in the great cosmopolitan cities of Instanbul, Rome, London, and New York, silent reminders that Thebes once ruled the world.

Scientific archaeology began in Egypt primarily with the work of English Egyptologist, Sir Flinders Petrie. He spent the years 1881-1924

Servants bring food of all kinds to their master and his wife. Note the legs of butchered animals, as well as vegetables, fruit and fowl. The women servants bring the delicately scented lotus blossoms. (About 19th century B.C.)

mostly in Egypt, developing the art of determining dates from pottery remains. His work has become the basis of our knowledge of ancient Egypt and has inspired hundreds of students and scholars.

During the 1920s many dramatic discoveries were made regularly by professional museum and university staffs, digging on a systematic and scientific basis. The world press was filled with exciting accounts of discovered relics from that ancient world. And in 1922 Howard Carter entered the untouched tomb of Tutankhamun. "King Tut" was an instant sensation.

Since that time, the treasures of Tutankhamun have outdrawn almost every other collection of art. Their beauty astounds a generation which is sophisticated enough to put men on the moon. We, whose lives are filled with moonshots, throwaway plastics, and fast foods, are awestruck by these 3,000-year-old splendors.

These are gold vessels found in the tombs of Egyptian princesses. (Lahun, about 19th century B.C.)

5

EGYPT
Gift of The Nile

A strand of papyrus which once grew in great abundance along the marshy banks of the Nile. Today most of the swamps have been drained, and the papyrus has almost disappeared from Egypt. It is still found in great quantities along the banks of the White and Blue Niles in the Sudan.

The Nile, timeless river of mystery, shaped the way of life in ancient Egypt, governing, to a large extent, the size and shape of the country. The cycles of the Nile's flooding set the rhythms of the Egyptian year.

The Nile included the triangle-shaped Delta and the long sinuous river that stretched 750 miles to the south from the Great Sea to the First Cataract. Egypt's land was the fertile soil (a few yards to a few hundred yards wide) on either side of the river. During some periods, Egypt extended further south along the banks of the river into Nubia and Kush as far as 300 miles south of the First Cataract. To the east and to the west of this narrow strip of fertile soil lay inhospitable deserts.

At times there were settlements in the great El Faiyum oasis. But it was primarily along the banks of the Nile that the ten million people of Egypt lived during the times of the pharaohs.

The Nile was like no other known river. For most of the year its clear waters flowed steadily northward from the heart of Africa. No rain fell on Egypt, apart from slight coastal showers along the shores of the Mediterranean Sea.

The source of these never-failing waters lay far south of Egypt, well beyond the knowledge of the Egyptians. They experienced this awesome flood without having an explanation for its cause. They attributed the Nile's annual rise to the will of the pharaoh, their god-king.

At a predictable moment each year in June, the water of the Nile changed color. It became muddy, rich with silt. The river began to rise above its banks and gradually fill the concave Nile Valley. The steadily swelling river actually reached its peak in September (early October in the Delta.)

The waters began to recede in late September. By November the river was back within its normal banks.

When the Nile was in full flood, it would reach hundreds of yards across. Rich layers of silt, left behind by the river's waters, rejuvenated the fertile soil to make Egypt one of the richest agricultural lands in the world. The

Reeds grew in profusion along the Nile's banks, affording rich feeding grounds for wild ducks. (Palace of Akhnaton, Tell el-Amarna, 14th century B.C.)

food raised on the Nile's life-giving deposits fed Egypt's people abundantly. It even provided surplus grain for export.

The Nile's Sources

The ancient Egyptians thanked their gods for the Nile. The sources of the Nile were never known to them, but remained for intrepid Victorian explorers to discover. One of the epic adventures of modern exploration was the nineteenth century discovery of the sources of the White Nile in the great lake system of Central Africa. These lakes collect water from the tropical heart of the continent and store it in a vast interlocked natural reservoir. The water starts its flow northward from Lakes Tanganyika, Kivu, Edward, George, Kwania, Kyga, and Victoria to funnel through remote Lake Albert. The water from the lakes pours out in a steady, clear stream. Instead of heading due east toward the Indian Ocean, a mere four hundred miles away, the White Nile starts its 4,000 mile-long course in a northerly direction, passing through the deserts of the Sudan and Egypt before it reaches the Mediterranean Sea.

The White Nile provides the steady year-round supply of water that keeps the Nile a full flowing river that never dries up.

The Blue Nile, named for the blue-gray silt which it carries in flood, is formed in the mountains of Ethiopia. The rains there are seasonal. The waters collect in mile-high Lake Tana and then overflow to cascade down, winding southward and westward through Ethi-

The Nile was rich in fish. Various fishing methods were used, including large nets, fixed nets, small hand-held nets, and line and hook. (Tomb of Mereruka, Sakkara, about 23rd century B.C.)

opia and then turning northward through the Sudanese desert to join the White Nile near modern Khartoum. The flood waters of the Blue Nile provide the added volume that causes the June to September flooding of the Egyptian fields over a thousand miles away.

Early Explorers

Early Egyptian explorers started from their base in the Delta, the rich alluvial fan where the Nile empties into the sea. This part of the Nile Valley, which extended through Lower Egypt, was called the Lower Nile. Leaving the Delta, explorers followed the Nile upstream. Hence the area upstream of the Delta was named the Upper Nile, or Upper Egypt. The prevailing winds blew to the south, so the Egyptians were able to sail their river craft upstream against the current, with the wind pushing them along. To come back downstream, they simply furled their sails and let the current carry them northward. If they wanted to make better time going downstream, they broke out oars.

They sailed upstream nearly 600 miles from the Delta without encountering any natural barrier. The Nile Valley was between two and twelve miles wide at any point, lined by limestone cliffs. For the most part, the fertile deposit of alluvial soil extended from between ten and two or three hundred yards on either side of the river bank. A sharp line could be seen between the desert and the fertile soil. Indeed a person could stand with one foot in a lush green crop and the other foot on barren desert. The villages were built of mud bricks and were usually located just beyond the normal boundaries where the fertile soil and the desert met.

At Edfu, the cliffs lining the valley changed to sandstone and ran closer along the river banks for another seventy miles. This sandstone provided building materials for the fabulous temples of Egypt.

Travelers going south then reached the first of six cataracts or extensive areas of rapids. In these areas the river crossed eroded ridges of hard rock. Travel by boat was dangerous in flood waters. Bypass slips around the worst of the rapids were made for the boats to use in time of low water. These slips were lined with mud from the Nile's bed. When water was sprinkled on the mud slip just in front of the boat, it became so slick that there was almost no friction and the boat slid along with little effort. Building blocks for great temples also were moved in this relatively effortless manner.

The Egyptians numbered these cataracts as they came to them, traveling from the north. The First is near modern Aswan. In ancient Egypt there were two beautiful islands, Elephantine and Philae, which marked the beginning of the cataract. Elephantine was the border city that marked the southernmost border of Upper Egypt and the beginning of Lower Nubia to the south. Nubia, like Egypt, was divided by the ancients into Lower and Upper Nubia. Nubia was the land along the Nile between the First and Sixth Cataracts. Its people and history were closely linked with the Egyptians across the centuries of pharaonic rule. Lower Nubia, the land between the First and Third Cataracts, is now under the waters of Lake Nasser, the huge reservoir created by the High Dam at Aswan.

Between the First Cataract and the Delta, the river falls through several hundred feet. This important geographical fact means that the water moves steadily onward as it flows to the seas, even when it is in full flood. Had the river bed been flatter, the water would have stagnated as the flood receded, drying in the sun and making the alluvial deposit saline and therefore infertile.

The rate of the water's fall also made primitive irrigation relatively easy. Water could be drawn off into an irrigation canal upstream from a field, run through the crop-bearing field by gravity, and easily drained back into the main stream of the river—only to be used again by another farmer downstream.

The rate of fall also kept the main river channel from silting up until the river reached the Delta. This fact, together with the direction of the prevailing wind and the steady supply of water in the river, made the Nile the chief highway of ancient Egypt. So convenient was the mode of travel that many people are recorded as having property both in the Delta and in the far reaches of Upper Egypt 500 miles upriver.

The fact that the Nile annually renewed the land next to its banks along a 650-mile course meant that Egypt was in effect a single farm, approximately 100 to 400 yards wide and 650 miles long, plus the Delta. The most efficient kind of government for such an ecological system would be a strong central one capable of administering water resources, collecting food in good years, and distributing it in lean ones. And that is just the kind of government that developed in early pharaonic times. Under the god-king, an elaborate bureaucracy developed to manage irrigation, collect taxes in the form of foodstuffs, and pay wages, also in the form of foodstuffs.

A Rural Nation

The nation was essentially rural and agricultural. Small villages dotted the valley just beyond fringes of the alluvial deposits—that rich soil was too precious to waste as a mere building site. The people lived out their lives in the vicinity of their village, following the annual round of farming under generally pleasant and easy conditions. The reliability of the Nile's cycles and

Famine due to low floods, locusts or blight was felt most quickly in the deserts. Here is an emaciated herdsman from the Libyan desert. (About 1900 B.C.)

9

the general abundance of crops contributed to the essentially conservative nature of the Egyptian. The old ways were tried and true, and not too arduous. It was considered best to repeat them each year, for the results were predictable.

Life along the Nile was so pleasant and happy that the Abode of the Dead, often thought of as being to the west—where the sun went down— was conceived as a continuation of everyday life. In some cultures, where life is harsh, the prevailing views of the afterworld are of a state for the dead which is totally different from that experienced by the living. In contrast, the Egyptian enjoyed his life so much that he wanted it continued in the blessed Western World of the Dead.

If a person went away from his village for a time, as a drafted soldier or a worker on some royal project, he usually returned to his village by the Nile. Life was regular, peaceful, and gentle. Friends and family had roots there that went back for centuries. The gods of the place were familiar and had sustained the family and the land from the beginning of time. The ancient Egyptian was at heart a satisfied, conservative Nile village farmer.

The government established a series of measuring stations or "nilometers" at many points along the river. If the flood was lower than average one year, food supplies would diminish at a predictable level depending on the actual height of the flood. If the flood was low several years running, the result was severe famine in the land. If, on the other hand, the flood was higher than average, villages would have to be warned to build dykes of reinforced mud bricks to keep the water from washing away the houses.

If the dykes were breached, the village would disappear since generally no stone was used in construction. The water would dissolve the dried mudbrick houses. But such an event was not an overwhelming catastrophe, since the houses could be easily rebuilt from the Nile mud as the waters subsided.

When the waters started to rise at Elephantine in June, measurements were carefully taken and the data rushed to the pharaoh. The rate of the water's rising was compared with records which had been kept across the years. The

The papyrus plant provided the building materials to make fishing boats in ancient Egypt. Fishermen hauled a net between two such crafts. (Models from the tomb of Neketre, Thebes, 21st century B.C.)

pharaoh and his administrators could predict the height the waters would reach that year and could forecast the economic consequences.

The height of the flood actually depended on the amount of rain that had fallen weeks before in the Ethiopian highlands. The Egyptians had no way of knowing how much had fallen, and so they waited for the results of the nilometer measurements with much anxiety. Usually low floods were more common than high floods.

Control of the flood level was the devout aim of every government. Thus in the early pharaonic era, a huge reservoir was created in a natural depression to the west of the Nile Valley. This lake measured 150 square miles and nearly filled the great El Faiyum Depression south of Memphis. An elaborate canal system in that vast area also reclaimed thousands of tillable acres from the desert.

The Nilotic Year

The calendar, based on 365 days in the solar year, was closely related to the cycles of the Nile. The Nilotic year began with the period of inundation (late June to October). This was followed by a period of sowing (late October to February). Then came the harvest period (March to early May). The last period (mid-May to mid-June) was one in which the river fell to its lowest level and the sun burned hottest. The fields dried out fully, even cracking open. Agricultural work mostly stopped. It was the time for work on national projects, such as temple building, until the Nile began to rise again and the farmers were required back in their fields for another season.

The wondrous fertility of Egypt can be sensed by noting the crops that were sown and harvested throughout the year:

Month	Sown	Bloom	Harvest
November	wheat	narcissus violets cassia trees	dates plum
December		wheat grasses flowers	
January	lupine beans flax	oranges pomegranates wheat (Upper Egypt)	sugar cane senna clover
February	rice	cabbages cucumbers melons	barley
March			wheat
April	winter wheat	roses	wheat clover (second crop)
May		acacia henna	winter wheat grapes figs carob dates
June			sugar cane (Upper Egypt)
July	rice		flax grapes
August	water lily jasmine		clover (third crop) melons dates grapes
September			oranges lemons tamarinds olives rice
October	new sowing season begins		

11

This wall painting shows the variety of food served in the houses of the wealthy. A garland of lotus blossoms crowns the abundance of poultry, fish, fruit, vegetables, and spices. (Tomb of Nakht, 15th century B.C.)

Cranes regularly nested in the Nile marshes. They were caught, fattened, and considered a delicacy for eating. (Tomb of Tiy, Sakkara, about 25th century B.C.)

Ancient paintings show more than one hundred varieties of birds, many of them caught for eating. The Nile marshes drew birds by the millions. There were also more than one hundred types of animals depicted, and an equal number of kinds of fish.

The Nile was rich in varieties of grasses and trees, including the highly prized lotus and papyrus. The lotus, symbol of Lower Egypt, was loved for its beauty and scent. People are often depicted holding a lotus bloom to their face, breathing in its perfume. The papyrus was the most useful of reeds, and made into items as diverse as paper and river punts.

Surrounding Deserts

If the Nile gave life to the people of Egypt, the surrounding deserts gave security. To the west was the end-less Libyan desert. It was a place of drifting dunes, of Bedouin caravan tracks, of oases fed by underground waters from the Nile. The only threat from across those wastelands came in the form of marauding bands of nomads, whose raids on camel back could be swift and ferocious. But there were no major nations with disciplined armies to march against Egypt from the west. Border outposts at key caravan points were usually adequate to provide Egypt with security on that frontier.

To the east of the Nile lay rugged, inhospitable mountains which rose as high as 7,000 feet in the 150 miles or so that separated the river from the Red Sea. No invading army from Asia could march across the heart of the Sinai Peninsula, ferry across the Red Sea, scale the rugged mountain barriers to descend on the Nile Valley. Wild animals, often sport for the pharaohs and his nobles, were the only natural inhabitants of that bleak area.

At Thebes, where an eastward bend in the river brings the Nile to just under one hundred miles from the Red Sea, a caravan track led to the sea. There was a port for shipping to the southern coasts of Africa and to parts of Asia.

Transport across the deserts, usually by camel caravan, was fully adequate for vigorous trade throughout the period of ancient Egypt. Many items have

The dove was a popular subject in Egyptian art. Here one is shown in a papyrus strand along the Nile. (Palace of Akhnaton, Tell el-Amarna, 14th century B.C.)

been found in tombs which came from Libya and Asia. The only significant military invasions Egypt ever faced came across the northern tip of the Sinai desert.

Lower Egypt (the Delta) was noticeably different from Upper Egypt (the Nile Valley). The Delta began at Heliopolis and fanned out from there in the shape of an inverted triangle until it reached the Mediterranean Sea 100 miles to the north. The wide top of this huge triangle stretched for 150 miles along the coastline. The Nile divided into seven main channels and five secondary ones, plus numerous canals and streams. The soil was wet and intensely fertile. Travel across Lower Egypt could take place only with extensive use of small ferryboats.

The Nile Gave Unity to Upper Egypt

The Nile gave to Upper Egypt a unity that ran for 650 miles along the river. Eventually this unity was focused in the royal seat at Thebes. Lower Egypt, however, was divided into dozens of sections by the river's branches, with strong local loyalties to gods and local nobles persisting for centuries.

Upper Egypt was rich in grain, Lower Egypt in grasses and in cattle. Irrigation was considerably easier in Lower Egypt, where garden crops, therefore, were always available. During those times when the central government was weak, life was easier and less disrupted in Lower Egypt because each section was more self-contained. The irrigation systems in the Nile Valley required much greater centralized management than did those in the Delta. The majority of ancient Egyptians lived in the Delta area, but the seats of power were in the hands of the southerners.

To the north of Lower Egypt was the Mediterranean Sea. For centuries, this sea, like the deserts, was a trade highway rather than an invasion route. Trade links were clearly established with Phoenicia, Syria, the Minoans on Crete, and possibly with Greece.

Ancient Egypt's most active frontier was on the Nile itself far to the south. Beyond Elephantine at the First Cataract lay Nubia, Kush, Punt, and the heart of black Africa. Trade was always active up and down the far reaches of the Nile. At times Egypt extended her borders southwards to include Nubia and Kush as far as the Fourth Cataract. Nubians were sometimes seen as potential invaders, sometimes as captured slaves, sometimes as trusted gendarmerie. And for one period of seventy years, the ruling pharaohs were Nubians (the Twenty-fifth Dynasty).

The primary invasion route against Egypt was up the Nile from the south. The Egyptians built a series of powerful fortifications in Nubia along the Nile to control access to Egypt, to guard vital trade routes, and to serve as

The fowler has baited his snare with seed and is waiting for the birds to spring the trap shut. (Tomb at Beni-hasan, about 1900 B.C.)

The Egyptians often trained wild animals that lived along the reaches of the Nile. Here a Nubian holds a trained cheetah which was probably used by the pharaoh for hunting in the desert. (Tomb of Rekhmire, Thebes, 15th century B.C.)

major trading posts directly under the pharaoh's management. These forts are now covered by the waters of Lake Nasser, which has backed up through most of Nubia behind the High Dam at Aswan.

Some temples which were originally built along the Nile in Nubia have been moved to higher ground, as in the case of the magnificent Abu Simbel temple built by Ramses II. Other temples have been carefully dismantled piece by piece and moved to other locations entirely, there to be reconstructed. Such is the case with the exquisite Dendun temple which is now at the Metropolitan Museum of Art in New York City's Central

Park. Yet other temples and the remains of forts are now covered by Lake Nasser, after standing for more than 3,000 years along the Nile.

If the river provided life and renewal to Egypt, and the land was a pleasant and secure one, it was the sun that dominated each day. There was no rain in the country, except for scattered coastal showers along the Mediterranean. Every day the sun rose large in the east out of the desert. It would move across the deep blue sky, now and then hidden in part by an occasional cloud which soon vanished. The sun settled, large and red, into the Libyan desert to the west.

At night, the Egyptians thought, the sun was swallowed by the sky-goddess. It passed through her body to be born again in the morning far to the east, only to move once more through the endless cycle of lighting the sky and warming the earth.

It was little wonder that the sun came to represent the chief of the gods.

For one brief moment during the reign of Pharaoh Akhnaton, all the panoply of Egypt's hundreds of gods and goddesses was banished. Only the sun was worshipped, as the god Aton, who was held to be the one true god.

The river, the land, and the sun, fused together in daily and annual rhythms, were the unchanging basics of Egyptian life throughout the era of the pharaohs. Those timeless cycles have been changed only in the last decade by the control of the flooding of the Nile's waters by the mighty Aswan High Dam.

Stone was used primarily in the construction of temples and monuments, not homes or even palaces. Here are remains of the pillars in a temple for the god Amun at Luxor, on the site of ancient Thebes. (14th century B.C.)

During the height of New Kingdom imperalism, foreign princes came to the pharaoh to present their gifts and tribute. This picture is from the tomb of the high priest of Amun during the reign of Thutmose III, the pharaoh who took his armies to the banks of the Euphrates River. The princes are described as being from Crete, Hatti (Hittite), Tunis, and Crete (left to right). The child being held is possibly a royal hostage. (Tomb of Menkheperreseneb, Thebes, 15th century B.C.)

EGYPT
From Menes To Cleopatra

For 3,000 years, with only relatively minor interruptions, Egypt was ruled by pharaohs. Although much older in time, this period of rule equals in length the record of the historic dynasties of China from the start of the Chou dynasty in 1122 B.C. to the fall of the Ching dynasty in 1911 A.D.

The word "pharaoh" came into use in New Kingdom times (c. 1500 B.C.) and is one of the many titles of the king. It means "He of the Great House." The rulers of the New Kingdom were renowned throughout the world for their glory and power. The term "pharaoh" came to be used to refer to all the rulers who preceded the New Kingdom titans, as well as those who followed. Many of the accounts in the Bible of early relations between the Hebrew people and Egypt were written about New Kingdom times. The pharaoh of the biblical Exodus may well have been Ramses II, a New Kingdom ruler. It was only natural that the term "pharaoh" was used in the biblical record to refer to the Egyptian king. This fact has helped popularize the use of the term in many languages and cultures around the world which have had only the Bible in translation as their sole point of contact with ancient Egypt.

More than 3,000 years passed between the first pharaoh and the last, in which time thirty-one dynasties of pharaohs ruled. A few of the notable pharaohs are discussed in this chapter. There is also a chronology which sets forth the dynasties, the major periods and individuals, and notable events.

The earliest traces of people living in Egypt go back to neolithic remains dating from about 5000 B.C. These remains are mostly flint instruments. Pottery, carved ivory figures, and slate palettes (used for mixing cosmetics) have been found buried with later peoples. The skill used in fashioning these artifacts shows a growing sophistication among pre-dynastic Egyptians.

Eventually some villages became larger and formed cities of a few thousand inhabitants. The chief of these cities exercised control over the surrounding area. In time there was a paramount chief who became ruler of all of Lower Egypt, and another who ruled over Upper Egypt. The unification of these two kingdoms or lands became the primary event of ancient Egyptian history.

The king of Lower Egypt wore a red crown. The symbols of the land were a bee and the papyrus. The king of Upper Egypt wore a white crown. The symbol of the land was the lotus blossom.

It is generally agreed that Menes was the first man to unite the Two Lands into a single kingdom. He was a southern king who conquered the north. He joined the emblematic crowns together in an ingenious design to form the new double crown of united Egypt.

Balance of the Two Lands

After his unification of Lower and Upper Egypt, Menes saw that if they were linked together in harmony, it would secure the prosperous future of both. So he established his new capital, which he called Memphis, at a neutral site close to the border of Lower Egypt. This reconciling gesture was successful. Memphis became known as the "balance of the Two Lands." Over the next few generations southern kings married northern princesses to forge ever closer ties between the two peoples.

From the time of unification on, there would always be both a northern and a southern center of governmental administration. The posts of royal governor or vizier in each of the Two Lands was so important that the vizier was often a member of the ruling pharaoh's immediate family. The continuance of this duplicate administration is evidence, across many centuries, of a deep-seated Egyptian awareness that the one nation had been formed out of the Two Lands.

Identifying the Pharaohs

Identifying the dates and even the names of many of the early pharaohs is impossible at the present time. Each ruler had several official and personal names. He was known by different names in different lists of rulers compiled by the ancients at different times. Egyptologists have not as yet succeeded in unravelling all this data in a manner which meets universal acceptance.

Menes' unification of Egypt is usually dated at about 3200 B.C. A period of settling and consolidation followed unification. The unity of the kingdom had to be reaffirmed by force a number of times. There were campaigns against Nubia in the south. A military presence was established in the strategic valley of the Second Cataract. Marauding bands of Bedouins to the east had to be neutralized; military forays against the Libyans to the west stabilized those borders.

After 500 years of consolidation, a series of able kings provided an era of stability in which a remarkable cultural flowering took place. This tranquil age has become known as the Old Kingdom. During the half-century from 2700 B.C. to 2180 B.C., the land knew peace. A powerful central government guaranteed security and fostered prosperity. The rulers were regarded as incarnate deities whose power was absolute. They were patrons of the crafts and the arts. The paintings and statuary from the Old Kingdom show a tranquility of spirit, an inner confidence, and a sense of place Egyptian art has not yet duplicated.

The Old Kingdom was seen by succeeding generations as the Golden Age, when Egypt was at her best. Its art became the models that were emulated, but never matched, even by artists in the time of the Ptolemies 2,000 years later.

Three Outstanding Pharaohs

Three names stand out from Old Kingdom times. The first is Pharaoh Djoser, who ordered the construction of the first of the great pyramids. The famous Step Pyramid, so named because the blocks were assembled in rising steps, unlike the later smooth-faced pyramids, was built in an area west of Memphis called Sakkara. Sakkara became the major monument and burial location for Old Kingdom rulers and nobles. Indeed, the tomb paintings of everyday life in the homes of the wealthy, of the field activities of the large manors, of the leisure pastimes of the nobility, all show a vital force and loving realism that was never matched again.

The second name is Imhotep. He was the official who carried out Djoser's wishes. He was so original in thought and in his practical application of theoretical mathematics that he stands in the forefront of the world's greatest intellectuals. The pyramid he built was probably the very first monument in history built in stone. What other human work has lasted almost intact for nearly 5,000 years?

Besides being an architect, mathematician, administrator, and engineer, Imhotep was renowned for founding Egyptian medicine, an art in which Egypt led the world for millennia, until their learning was passed on to their Arab successors. Imhotep also was noted among the ancients as the father of Egyptian magic and astronomy.

The recitation of the proper magical formulas was essential for enabling a dead person to pass safely into the blessed Western World of the Dead. Astronomy was put to essential use in

The nearest pyramid was built by Pharaoh Khaefre, the second by his successor, Pharaoh Menkaure. These pyramids were built at a time when the Pharaoh was absolute monarch, combining in himself all the powers of god and king. (Giza, 27th century B.C.)

19

forecasting the seasons of the Nile's flooding. Ancient Egypt developed the world's first solar calendar. The pyramids were laid out on a true north–south axis, perhaps for some magical-religious reason related to the worship of the sun-god. The Egyptians even discovered a method by which they accurately measured the circumference of the earth. This was through sun measurements taken on the Tropic of Cancer at noon on the day of the summer solstice.

The security and conservatism of Egypt's stable society fostered the honoring and remembering of great men. Because of this, Imhotep's name reaches us out of the distant past as the first genius to be known by name.

The third name to come to us from the Old Kingdom is Pharaoh Khufu. The Greeks called him Cheops. It was he who built the largest pyramid at Giza, a short distance downriver from Sakkara. His son, Khaefre, also built a massive pyramid and the awesome Sphinx.

The Old Kingdom Decline

The Old Kingdom ended in a period of social confusion, decay, and anarchy. Egyptologists have called this the First Intermediate Period. All the stable virtues based on the timelessness of the god-king ruler collapsed as centralized government itself disappeared. The exact reasons for this decline are not known. There was famine, and social unrest broke out in riots and led to class revolution. A work entitled *Admonitions* by Ipuwer has survived from these days. It describes a world turned upside down: "He who possessed no property is now a man of wealth. The poor man is full of joy. Every town says: let us suppress the powerful among us. He who had no oxen is now possessor of land. The owners of robes are now in

Medicine was practiced with great skill. Imhotep, the Old Kingdom genius, was known as the Father of Medicine. Here a Syrian prince is being treated by an Egyptian doctor (Tomb of Nebamon, Thebes, 15th century B.C.)

rags. . . . The children of princes are dashed against the walls."*

Reunification of the government and the re-establishment of strong central rule came about 2040 B.C. under a pharaoh from Thebes. This event initiated another great age of culture and prosperity, called the Middle Kingdom. No longer were the god-kings considered faultless as they were in the height of Old Kingdom times. Now they had to worry over matters of state in which their powers were shared with strong nobles (called nomarchs) whose bases were the major cities and their surrounding regions (called nomes). The faces of the statues of Middle Kingdom pharaohs show signs of this struggle of spirit which is not seen in the more tranquil Old Kingdom statuary.

Under Middle Kingdom pharaohs, Egyptian rule extended southward along the Nile below the Second Cataract to include Kush. The mountains and deserts on either side of the Nile in Nubia and Kush became the source of Egypt's great wealth in gold and semiprecious stones. Slaves, condemned prisoners, and prisoners of war—even children—were sent to mine the gold in subhuman conditions.

The Middle Kingdom faded into a second period of chaos, known as the Second Intermediate Period. Toward the end of this period, Semitic invaders from the Middle East seized control of Lower Egypt. These Asiatic invaders, called Hyksos, established a dynasty of pharaohs. It was perhaps while this dynasty was in power that the Hebrew Joseph came to Egypt as a slave and rose to the position of vizier, as recorded in the Book of Genesis.

The Hyksos ruled for over a century, extracting regular tribute from the Egyptian nobles (nomarchs) in Upper Egypt. One of the major innovations brought to Egypt by the Hyksos was the two-horse war chariot.

In time the nomarchs of southern Egypt rallied around a prince of Thebes. He and his son led a war of liberation against the Hyksos and drove them out

of the land by developing superior tactical use of the chariot. Under these two men, Kamose and his son Ahmose, the Two Lands were reunited again under a native Egyptian pharaoh.

The capital was moved from near Memphis to Thebes. The Theban pharaohs could readily keep track of events up the Nile in Nubia and Kush, as well as down the Nile to the Delta and Libyan desert beyond the El Faiyum oasis and reservoir. The chief god of Thebes became the chief god of the pharaoh and of the land.

New Kingdom Greatness

Once the borders were secure again and stable rule was restored throughout the land, Egypt entered another age of greatness, called the New Kingdom. During this period the wealth of the pharaoh was measured in Nubian gold. Asiatic vassals or rulers of client states wrote to ask the pharaoh for quantities of gold, since they had little and he was known to have so much. The pharaoh's army was manned by large numbers of Nubian troops. The national police force was essentially a Nubian constabulary under command of a Nubian captain who reported directly to the pharaoh.

Nubia became so fully integrated with Egypt that one of the most widely known New Kingdom pharaohs, Ramses II, had a large temple, which was dedicated primarily to himself and the chief gods Re-Harakti, Ptah, and Amun, carved into the very cliffs of Nubia at Abu Simbel between the First and Second Cataracts. The pharaoh's own son was often appointed viceroy over Nubia. He was called the King's Son of Kush, and carried the king's own signet ring.

The New Kingdom pharaohs built their tombs on the western side of the Nile across from Thebes in a deep valley, now called the Valley of the Kings. They built palaces for themselves on the eastern bank of the river. They constructed magnificent temple complexes on the western bank to honor the gods. Thebes, during the height of the New Kingdom, was the grandest city in the world.

*Jacquetta Hawkes, *The First Great Civilization* (New York: Alfred A. Knopf, 1973), p. 298.

This group of rulers comprise the major pharaohs of the New Kingdom. Here from the top left are Queen Hatshepsut, Thutmose III, Amenhotep III, Amenhotep IV (Akhnaton), and Tutankhamun. During the rule of these pharaohs Egypt expanded to its furthest extent and achieved its greatest wealth.

Several New Kingdom rulers have captured the imagination of the world because of their interesting lives and their monumental achievements.

One of the most interesting of such women of ancient history was Queen Hatshepsut. (Her statue appears on the cover of this book.) She was the official heiress of a pharaoh whose name was Thutmose I. The legitimacy of the pharaonic line normally passed through the eldest daughter of the Great Wife of a pharaoh to the man that daughter married. Hapshepsut was the only child of the Great Wife of Thutmose I.

Hatshepsut married the son of a secondary wife of Thutmose I, thus giving her husband legitimate right to rule as pharaoh. He ruled for a time as Thutmose II, and died leaving a daughter by Hatshepsut, his Great Wife. He had a son, also named Thutmose, by a concubine. This young boy was married to Hatshepsut's daughter, and thereby acquired the title of pharaoh.

However, Hatshepsut had different ideas. She, powerful personality and royal personage that she was, took over the rule of Egypt as regent. She was—all at the same time—dowager queen, mother-in-law, and half-aunt to the child-pharaoh. She enjoyed the full support of the high priest of Amun, the chief god of Thebes. Hatshepsut proclaimed herself king and assumed all the royal titles of a ruling pharaoh except that of "the Mighty Bull."

Her reign was glorious in cultural achievement and national well-being. After over twenty years as sole ruler, she shared the realm with her son-in-law, Thutmose III, as co-regent. When she died and he assumed full monarchical powers, one of his first acts was to have her name chiseled off all the inscriptions that described her achievements in all the temples and monuments she had erected. He had her name replaced by those of his grandfather (her father), his father (her husband), or himself.

Imperial Egypt

Under Thutmose I and especially under Thutmose III the New Kingdom pharaohs spread their power abroad towards the heart of Asia. Egypt became imperial Egypt. The armies of Thutmose III won victories in Asia over the Mitanni and other nations. He secured control of the land as far as the banks of the Euphrates River.

For over a century during New Kingdom times, the rulers of smaller vassal states in Syria, Palestine, and Phoenicia sent gifts to the pharaoh as recognition of his sway over them. The Assyrians, the Babylonians, and the Hittites sent gifts to placate the pharaoh and to help keep international peace. The Egyptian army stationed garrison troops throughout the Middle East. Marriages between the pharaoh and daughters of the rulers of Syria, Phoenicia, and other Asian subject states cemented Egyptian supremacy in this sphere of international influence.

Tribute, food, people, and wealth from Asia poured into Thebes, making it one of the greatest cosmopolitan centers of world civilization. The sons and daughters of the rulers of subject states were brought to Thebes at a very early age. On the one hand, they served as hostages to ensure cooperation from their families, on the other hand, they were educated in the Egyptian royal house as part of the pharaoh's own family. They became thoroughly Egyptianized in the process. When they were older, they were sent back home, having ingrained loyalties and cultural conditioning which led them to support Egypt's interest at an almost unconscious level. In many instances, Egypt placed a prince so educated on the foreign throne of his father.

England and France did something of the same thing in the nineteenth century by educating thousands of colonials in London and Paris. The similarity would have been greater had the English, for instance, taken foreign colonial princes directly into the English royal household for education and married them to members of the royal family.

Communications between Thebes and the far reaches of the empire were excellent. There was regular courier service on well-traveled trade and military roads. Official letters between Egyptian subjects in the Middle East and Thebes have survived. They were written in the Egyptian language, but on clay tablets using cuneiform. These letters contain matters of state between Thebes and the princes of Jerusalem, Byblos, Tyre, Sidon, Beirut, Askalon, Megiddo, and Accho.

Akhnaton and Nefertiti

One of the most fascinating of the New Kingdom rulers was Amenhotep IV, better known to history as Akhnaton. His wife was the stunningly beautiful Nefertiti. Amenhotep IV came to the throne when the empire was at its greatest extension and power. However, he was not very interested in foreign affairs, and Egyptian influence abroad suffered as a result of his negligence in managing the empire.

Amenhotep IV devoted his energies to the reform of the religious character of Egypt. He focused all his attention on a new form of the sun-god. He declared this new god, whom he called Aton, to be the only god, the source of all life. Under royal pressure, overt worship of all the other gods of Egypt was abandoned. A new holy city was built near Thebes, named after the god Aton. The pharaoh even changed his own name to include that of the god: he called himself Akhnaton—"He Who Is Beneficial to Aton." His monomania about Aton made him the world's first known monotheist.

The priesthoods and the temples of the scores of other Egyptian gods fell

Pharaoh Akhnaton and his Great Wife, Queen Nefertiti, are shown worshipping the sun god, Aton. One of their daughters stands behind the Queen. The sun's rays each end in a hand of blessing over the land. This example of Amarna Age art was often thought to be "grotesque" by scholars, but is rather a splendid early example of black African cultural influence on Egyptian art. (14th century B.C.)

into disrepute and disrepair. The priests never forgave Akhnaton for his official attack on their traditional religion and the threat he posed to their influence. When he died, they saw to it that the succeeding pharaoh, the boy Tutankhamun, returned to traditional religious orthodoxy. He restored the old gods, and contributed financially to the rebuilding of their temples and the support of their priesthoods. Once back in power, the priests tried to erase all trace of Akhnaton and his god. His holy city fell in ruin.

Akhnaton had built his holy city at a site near Thebes, now called Amarna. He fostered an artistic freedom of expression that broke all the customary rigidities of Old Kingdom classical form. There is a delightful sensuousness, realism, and humor to Amarna art. Akhnaton is shown as a loving father, engaged in the joys of family living, rather than as a formalized, austere demi-god.

Controversial Art

For years commentators called Amarna art "grotesque." Akhnaton is said to appear in portraits that "reveal his indolence of carriage, his haggard, unshapely body, his thick and flabby thighs, long neck, and grotesquely ugly facial features. . . . His figure was accepted as the ideal Egyptian type. . . . Thus, other Egyptians. . .were depicted as nearly like the king as possible. . .the prominent bodily peculiarities which nature had bestowed upon him became exaggerated yet more until they resulted in nothing less than veritable burlesque."* This was the considered judgement of many traditional Egyptologists, appearing even on museum labels next to Amarna paintings and reliefs.

An entirely different perspective surfaced at a major exhibition of Amarna art in 1973 at the Brooklyn Museum. Black visitors to the showing of the museum's superb Akhnaton and Nefertiti collection wrote their comments in a visitors' book. They "expressed

*George Steindorf and Keith P. Steele, *When Egypt Ruled the East* (Chicago and London: the University of Chicago Press, 1951), p. 219.

This magnificent inlaid picture of the throne of Tutankhamun. It was made, however, during the period when he still worshipped Aton, and his name was Tutankhaton. Note the sun with the rays ending in hands of blessing, a symbol of Aton, the sun-god espoused by Pharaoh Akhnaton. The Queen is the daughter of Akhnaton and wife of Tutankhamun. The art style is Amarna Age. (Tomb of Tutankhamun, 14th century B.C.)

delight at the apparent 'blackness' of the great Egyptian king, along with 'disgust and anger' at the museum's labels which drew attention to the 'grotesque and exaggerated' representation of his features, which they saw as being merely black."**

The later Twenty-fifth Dynasty of Egyptian pharaohs were indeed black Nubians. By New Kingdom times when Akhnaton ruled, Nubian and black African art traditions, as well as the people themselves, were fully absorbed into the Egyptian spirit. This is reminiscent of the way in which black American music has become a major influence on all contemporary American music.

Due to institutionalized and unconscious academic racism, Amarna art had not been appreciated for what it really was: the oldest expression of black artists known to mankind.

Akhnaton's children were all daughters, as a result of which Nefertiti fell into disrepute and was set aside. In desperation, he married one of his daughters in order to father a son. She bore him another daughter. When Akhnaton died, his successor was an eight- or nine-year-old boy.

This young ruler was married to Akhnaton's daughter-wife. The marriage insured the legitimacy of the young boy's claim to the throne. The boy-king's name was Tutankhaton. He was guided by strong courtiers who wantd to restore the older ways. During Akhnaton's reign foreign relations had deteriorated, and the monomania made the populace restive. So the boy-king's name was changed: "Aton" was dropped from it and he became known as Tutankhamun (in recognition of the traditional Theban god, Amun). The name means "Beautiful in Life is Amun."

He is so much better known to us than any other pharaoh because his was the one pharaonic tomb to survive intact. His tomb was discovered in 1922. The riches of his funerary collection rightly dazzle the modern

---

**Wendy Grabel, "The Brooklyn Museum Lands a 'Plum' in Job With Cairo Museum Renovation," *The Pheonix,* (Brooklyn, NY), March 16, 1978, p. 17.

viewer, coming as they do from the artistic height of Amarna creativity. They mirror the wealth of the New Kingdom at its height. Tutankhamun's reign was short and dominated by the strong men around the throne. Ironically, even much of his magnificent funerary equipment had been made for another young man who, had he lived, would have been pharaoh after Akhnaton instead of Tutankhamun.

Another well-known New Kingdom pharaoh was Ramses II. He was ambitious to extend Egypt's eastern border to the Euphrates, where it had been in earlier times. But by this time Hittite power had grown and compromises had to be reached with that warlike nation. Eventually the daughter of the Hittite king was given in marriage to Ramses II and raised above others in his harem to the place of "Great Wife." Instead of conquering the Hittites as previous pharaoh's had, Ramses II was obliged to come to terms with them through diplomacy. The power of the New Kingdom was fading, and Asian nations were beginning to sense themselves as the new center of world power.

As history shows, a nation's decline often signals an explosion of monumental building. This activity glorifies the state and its leaders. So it is no surprise that Ramses II was the most prolific builder in Egyptian history. He built temples, palaces, burial chambers, colossal statuary, cities, forts, memorial stelae and walls depicting his triumphs in dramatic (even if sometimes partly fictional) detail. The average Egyptian living in the Nile Valley probably would not have thought of this ceaseless activity as a sign of national decline, but in fact the next 1,100 years of pharaonic history was more or less a holding action against redundant internal pressures. The fact that pharaonic Egypt lasted so long at a time when other nations were rising to world-power status demonstrates the remarkable stability of its way of life and the security of its geographic location. The deeply conservative nature of Egypt and the basic well-being enjoyed by the peasant due to the rich bounty of the Nile gave this society a cohesion no other nation has ever experienced.

When Tutankhamun came to the throne he was a boy of eight or nine. The actual governing of Egypt fell to the aged vizier who had served under Akhnaton, a man by the name of Eye. In a few years, Eye was appointed co-regent with Tutankhamun. When the young king died at the age of eighteen, Eye was made sole king and ruled for about four years as pharaoh. He is the person who prepared the funerary furnishings of Tutankhamun's tomb. Here Pharaoh Eye is shown in a relief in his own tomb having a meal with Pharaoh Akhnaton. (Tomb of Eye, Thebes, 14th century B.C.)

The second in a series of coffins in which the body of Pharaoh Tutankhamun was laid. His tomb was discovered in 1922 by Howard Carter and is the only royal tomb discovered unmolested by early tomb robbers. This coffin shows Tutankhamun in the likeness of Osiris, the god of resurrection. Note the beard wig, a symbol of royalty, on the chin of the teen-aged pharaoh. The insert shows the mummified head of Tutankhamun. (14th century B.C.)

New Kingdom Wanes

At the end of the New Kingdom period, Egypt gave up her Asian territories. After that, she entered into the international political arena only from time to time to protect her eastern approaches. She felt safer when Syria and Palestine were in her sphere of influence, but this was seldom the case after New Kingdom times.

As the New Kingdom waned, the power of the priests grew in direct ratio to the decline of the king's power. The temples were by now major landholders. People seemed to become more religious as times grew more difficult, thus further increasing the authority of the priests.

Within the Royal House, harem intrigues contributed to struggles over

Ramses III is shown standing before the goddess Isis. The goddess says to the king, "I give you many years of life." The partially shown figure behind the king is his son, the crown prince. The words on the fan he holds are, "the crown prince who is over the two lands, the royal son, his beloved son." (12th century B.C.)

the inheritance of the throne. Some pharaohs had more than 150 children by scores of wives and concubines. Such a menage was not only costly and time-consuming for the pharaoh, but made strife inevitable between wives seeking to better the interests of their children. As the New Kingdom came to a close, the power of the ruling pharaoh was much less than it had been in the days either of the Imperial Kingship of a Ramses II or during the Divine Rule of Djoser.

The last of the Ramessid pharaohs was Ramses XI. He was overthrown in 1085 B.C. by the high priest of Amun. This event introduced what Egyptologists call the Late Period. There were times of peace and relative prosperity, followed by times of internal strife, economic turmoil, and invasion from foreign nations or plundering by desert tribes.

Libyan Pharaohs

In 940 B.C. Libyans seized the pharaonic throne, and they were to rule Egypt from the Delta area for over two hundred years. One of these Libyan pharaohs sacked the city of Jerusalem shortly after the rule of Solomon in Judea. The Bible records that Solomon had married one of the daughters of the pharaoh, possibly the first of these Libyan pharaohs, who wanted to reassert an Egyptian presence in Palestine. The alliance by marriage must have turned sour after Solomon died, for in the fifth year of the reign of his son, Rehoboam, "King Shishak of Egypt attacked Jerusalem. He took away all treasures in the Temple and in the palace, including the gold shields Solomon had made" (I Kings. 14:25-6).

In 712 B.C. Nubians took over the Egyptian state. Although the early pharaohs had feared Nubia more than any other nation, in time the Nubians became more Egyptian than the Egyptians. The older historic values were honored in Nubia, a Nilotic land of entrenched tradition. When the Nubians ruled Egypt, their aim was to reestablish all the old traditional ways. They were well into achieving their goals when foreign invasion toppled their dynasty.

Assyria, by then the dominant world power, invaded Egypt in 670 B.C.

A Libyan pharaoh, Shishak, sacked Jerusalem. Here a commemorative wall at Karnak tells of his triumphs in Judah and Israel. This wall is the southern wall of a temple to the god Amun. The main figure shown is Amun who holds strings attached to his prisoners, the rulers of more than 180 conquered cities. The name of the city is engraved in an oval on the body of the ruler. Other prisoners are seen at the right on bended knees and with raised arms indicating their submission. (10th century B.C.)

under Esarhaddon. The conquest of Egypt by Assyria was completed by Assurbanipal. He established a military government in Lower Egypt.

The Assyrian supply line was too long, and there were no sympathizers in Egypt to provide local support. The Assyrians were expelled from Egypt in 663 B.C. This was followed by a period of cultural renewal and national rediscovery. The art of the Old Kingdom was used as the model for artistic expression, but the work was clearly imitative.

Egypt's army played a role once more in the Asian power game, only to be crushed by the newest entry to the world-power sweepstakes, the emerging Persian Empire. Egypt was defeated in 525 B.C. by the Persians under Cambyses.

Egypt was made into a province or satrapy of the Persian Empire. The governors or satraps of Egypt took to themselves the title and ceremonial role of the pharaoh. They assumed the position of pharaoh vis-a-vis the Egyptian people, while remaining subject to the Persian king. Persian rule continued for nearly two hundred years. Occasionally one of the pharaohs during this period was an Egyptian; more often they were Persian.

The Persian Empire fell to Alexander the Great in 331 B.C. The next year he conquered Egypt. He founded the city of Alexandria on the Mediterranean just to the west of the Delta. Alexander was readily accepted as the new pharaoh and as the divine son of the god Amun.

Last Pharaonic Dynasty

When Alexander died of fever in Babylon in 323 B.C., his empire was divided among his generals. Egypt fell to Ptolemy Soter, who became pharaoh and established the last pharaonic dynasty, called the Ptolemaic Dynasty.

The Ptolemies ruled Egypt for three hundred years. They were Hellenistic in origin and culture. They made Alexandria into the world's cultural center, and the site of the ancient world's greatest library. Yet these Hellenists were also deeply affected by the traditions of the Egypt they ruled.

They carried on the pharaonic rules for inheritance of the throne. They became wholly absorbed in Egyptian mystery religion. They were mummified and buried as were the pharaohs of old, and their art reflected classical Egyptian tradition, though it had a Hellenistic overlay.

Queen Cleopatra

Queen Cleopatra was eighteen years old when she was enthroned as Cleopatra VII. This took place in 51 B.C. She had hoped to combine the wealth of Egypt, the culture and learning of Greece, and the strength of Rome to form a new world power with herself as queen. At first, she thought Julius Caesar was the means to realize this dream. So she became his mistress and bore his son, Caesarion.

Caesar, however, was assassinated. Cleopatra then saw in Anthony, one of Caesar's generals, the probable winner in the Roman power struggle that resulted. She married him and bore him children.

Anthony almost won control of Rome—if he had, Cleopatra would have been his queen. However, Anthony was defeated by the wily Octavian, who was later acclaimed as Augustus Caesar, at the battle of Actium in 31 B.C. Anthony fled to Alexandria, where, after a year of indecision, he committed suicide. Octavian occupied the city, taking Cleopatra prisoner. He planned to take her to Rome to show her as a captive in a great celebration of his triumph.

Rather than submit to such humiliation—going to Rome as a captive in custody rather than as queen of the ruling Caesar—Cleopatra cleverly arranged a private visit to Anthony's tomb. She committed suicide there by inducing a fatal bite from an asp which had been brought to her in the tomb in a basket filled with fruit.

Although she had foiled Octavian's plan to show her in a triumphal parade in Rome, her death meant that Octavian was free to loot the Ptolemy treasury. The riches of the Ptolemies, a burdensome taxation levied on the Egyptians, and the continuing wealth of the fertile Nile Valley enabled Octavian to pay his legionnaires well, thus assuring their loyalty to him. From that time on, he was personally wealthy, and thus able to be independent of the Roman Senate for the rest of his life.

When Cleopatra died, 3,000 years of pharaonic rule ended. Egypt became a Roman province. In the following centuries, she was ruled in succession by the Romans, the Byzantines, the Islamic Caliphate, the Fatimids, the Ayyubids, the Mamelukes, the French, and the British, until modern Egypt gained independence in 1922. The present republic was instituted in 1953.

The priesthoods became powerful in later New Kingdom times. Here Neferhotep, the chief scribe of the god Amun and superintendent of the oxen and heifers of Amun, is being driven in his chariot. Two men with staves keep the people following the chariot from getting too close. A Nubian herald runs before to announce Neferhotep's coming. Women and children greet the great man with dancing and music. Through their diaphanous gowns the women's legs can be seen dancing. Neferhotep wears a golden collar which might have been presented to him by the pharaoh. (Tomb of Neferhotep, Thebes, 13th century B.C.)

Highlights of Ancient Egyptian History

B.C. Date	Dynasty	Principal Rulers	Principal Events
(Dates are approximate.)			

PREHISTORIC

B.C. Date	Dynasty	Principal Rulers	Principal Events
Before 3200			Stone age hunters Agriculture along the Nile and in the Delta
			Kings in Lower and Upper Egypt

ARCHAIC PERIOD

B.C. Date	Dynasty	Principal Rulers	Principal Events
3200	I	Menes traditionally the first ruler of unified Egypt (8 rulers)	Royal tombs built at Abydos and Sakkara Founding of Memphis as capital city
2850	II	(9 rulers)	Stone masonry first used in burial chambers

THE OLD KINGDOM

B.C. Date	Dynasty	Principal Rulers	Principal Events
2700	III	Djoser (5 rulers)	Step Pyramid (first stone pyramid) Stone used for first time extensively for buildings and statuary

B.C. Date (Dates are approximate.)	Dynasty	Principal Rulers	Principal Events
2600	IV	Khufu (Cheops) Khaefre (6 rulers)	Great pyramids built at Giza Khaefre built the sphinx at Giza Copper and gold mining and smelting in Nubia and Phoenicia Height of sacred pharaonic power Highest level of art and literature
2500	V	(9 rulers)	High level of sculpture Great stability and prosperity Trading expeditions to Punt (Somalia?) Use of religious texts in burial chambers
2340	VI	Pepi II	Longest reign of any ruler in history (90 years as pharaoh) Decline of centralized state

FIRST INTERMEDIATE PERIOD

2180	VII-VIII		Weak kings in Memphis Asiatics control Delta at times
2100	IX-X		State breaks up into warring city-states (or nomes) Eastern frontiers re-established Thebes begins to rise in power

B.C. Date (Dates are approximate)	Dynasty	Principal Rulers	Principal Events
			Time of general social, religious, and kingly deterioration

THE MIDDLE KINGDOM

B.C. Date	Dynasty	Principal Rulers	Principal Events
2134	XI		Several Theban kings ruling during the same time as the last of the Xth dynasty ruler.
		Menthuhotep I	Two Lands reunited under Theban ruler
			Major irrigation projects, especially in El Faiyum
			Campaigns in south into Kush
2000	XII	Amenemhet I (8 rulers)	Restoration of peace and prosperity
			Major fortified trading posts in Nubia and Kush
			Trade with Syria and Crete
			Campaigns in Palestine
			Centralized government fully restored

SECOND INTERMEDIATE PERIOD

B.C. Date	Dynasty	Principal Rulers	Principal Events
1780	XIII–XIV	Many petty rulers	Collapse of central government
1700	XV–XVI	Hyksos rulers (6 rulers)	Conquest of Lower Egypt by the Hyksos, who were an Asiatic Semitic people and who introduced the chariot and iron to Egypt

B.C. Date (Dates are approximate.)	Dynasty	Principal Rulers	Principal Events
1600	XVII	Kamose	War of liberation; expulsion of the Hyksos
			Rise of Theban rulers

THE NEW KINGDOM

1570	XVIII	Ahmose	Complete expulsion of the Hyksos
1500	XVIII	Hatshepsut	Nubian gold and slaves; African goods are the key to Egypt's great wealth
			Southern frontier extended to Fourth Cataract
			Capital at Thebes; great period of temple building across the river from Thebes
		Thutmose III	Campaigns in Asia extended borders of empire to the Euphrates River
1400		Amenhotep III	Peak of imperial expansion and time of greatest wealth
			Rise of Theban god Amun
		Amenhotep IV (Akhnaton)	Period of the Aton "heresy"
			Capital relocated to Amarna
			Amarna Age in art, combined influences of Egypt, Asia, and black Africa
			Feud between priests and Akhnaton

B.C. Date (Dates are approximate.)	Dynasty	Principal Rulers	Principal Events
			Asiatic states in revolt
		Tutankhamun	Restores capital to Thebes and reinstitutes worship of Amun and traditional gods
		(16 rulers)	Fall of the Minoan kingdom and rise of the Hittites
1310	XIX	Ramses II	Attempts made to restore the fading Empire
			Asian campaigns
			Capital moved to Delta area to be closer to Asian affairs
		(9 rulers)	Great building activity, including Abu Simbel in Nubia
1184	XX	Ramses III	Ruler's powers and prestige steadily decline as priests' powers rise
			Hittites fade as world power
		Ramses IV-XI	Loss of Asian subject states
			Rise of priestly power

THE LATE PERIOD

B.C. Date (Dates are approximate.)	Dynasty	Principal Rulers	Principal Events
1080	XXI	(7 rulers)	Kings rule in Lower Egypt
			Priests rule in Upper Egypt
940	XXII	Libyan rulers	Nubia and Kush independent

B.C. Date (Dates are approximate.)	Dynasty	Principal Rulers	Principal Events
	XXIII	Libyan rulers (12 rulers)	Pharaoh Shishak plunders Jerusalem temple
730	XXIV	(2 rulers)	Growth of Assyrian power
712	XXV	Nubian rulers (5 rulers)	Attempt to restore lost Egyptian virtues and practices by Nubian rulers
			Upper and Lower Egypt reunited
			Nubian rule broken by Assyrian invasion
			During short period of Assyrian rule, Thebes was sacked by Assyrians
663	XXVI	Psamtik I	Expels Assyrians
		(6 rulers)	Trade established with Greece
525	XXVII-XXXI	Persian rulers with some weak Egyptian puppet rulers	Cambyses the Persian
			Egypt was under Persian rule, except for a short period when the Greeks helped win a brief interlude of independence

THE GRAECO-ROMAN PERIOD

B.C. Date	Dynasty	Principal Rulers	Principal Events
332	XXXII	Alexander the Great	Alexander conquers Egypt, enthroned as pharaoh, founds Alexandria
			End of native Egyptian rule
323	XXXIII	Ptolemy Soter	Alexandria becomes world cultural center

B.C. Date (Dates are approximate.)	Dynasty	Principal Rulers	Principal Events
		Cleopatra VII (15 rulers)	Last of the rulers with the title of pharaoh (died 30 B.C.)
30			Egypt becomes a Roman province

EGYPT
People at Home

Egyptian women normally wore white linen gowns, sometimes with colorful gold and stone collars.

The majority of Egyptian homes were built of sun-dried mud bricks. Wood was scarce, used only for a few pieces of furniture and for posts at doorways and windows. Stone was reserved for temples, funerary buildings, and parts of the homes of the very wealthy.

In the kitchen, women cooked by fires made from papyrus roots. Sometimes they burned chaff, date-stones, or dried cattle dung.

Women normally ground their own grain, using mostly wheat and barley. Each kitchen had its own grinding stone. The women baked a wide, tasty variety of breads and cakes, usually baked on top of a hot stone rather than in an oven. The bread was similar in shape and texture to the popular *pita* or Syrian bread still widely used in Egypt and the Middle East. In larger, wealthier homes, men as well as women worked as bakers and cooks.

The Egyptians used grain to brew an excellent beer. They prized beer highly and made a variety of brews, each with its own name and special season for drinking. They also made a fine wine from the fruit of date and palm trees.

The best wine, however, came from extensive vineyards, especially in Lower Egypt and the El Faiyum. The Egyptians identified the best wines by sealing them in earthen jugs and labeling the seal with the name of the vineyard owner, the name of the chief gardener, and the year of the vintage. Wine was costly. It was beyond the reach of the average person, who was quite content with his generous portions of locally brewed beer.

The grape harvest was a time of great joy. Sometimes the picked grapes were wrapped in a large linen cloth which was then twisted at both ends, the juice being collected in a vat. But the best grapes were pressed by treading on them with bare feet in a large vat. After the wine fermented, it was brought out in jars and there was a celebration. The jars were decorated with

(Above) *In New Kingdom times, men's dress went from the ankle to the waist, with a short-sleeved shirt. The use of pleats indicate wealth and social position. Here envoys from Asia are doing obeisance to Pharaoh Tutankhamun and presenting gifts to him. They are being presented by a court official. (Tomb near Thebes, 14th century* B.C.*)*

(Left) *A beautiful colored limestone statue of a servant grinding wheat in a hand mill. She wears a wig to keep the dust out of her hair. (Giza, about 25th century* B.C.*)*

Egyptian men were usually clean shaven. Here barbers are at work shaping the hair. (Tomb at Beni-hasan, 19th century B.C.)

Here are a shawl, a kerchief, and a dress made of fine linen. The cloth has been preserved because of the very dry climate in Egypt.

garlands of flowers and bunches of grapes, and there was much singing and dancing.

Simplicity of Clothes

Egyptians generally wore linen, made from the flax which grew so abundantly along the Nile. The lines of their clothes were very simple in Old Kingdom times. They became more elaborate by mid-New Kingdom times with the clever use of a variety of pleats and folds. The linen was bleached white. One of the characteristics of Asian foreigners which intrigued the Egyptian artists was the Asian art of dying woolen cloth with bright colors. Intrigued as they were with this exotic show of finery, however, the Egyptians did not copy those foreign styles to any extent.

Men generally wore a very simple wrap-around that extended from the waist to mid-thigh. It was held together by tucking the ends in around the waist or by using a decorative belt. In later times, wealthy men wore a wrap-around that extended down to their ankles, and sometimes wore a loose-fitting short-sleeved linen shirt that pulled over their heads.

The women wore a loose

A hairdresser works on her mistress's hair. The hieroglyphic inscription reads: "The hairdresser Inu." (21st century B.C.)

The Great Wife of Ramses II is seen wearing an elegant, diaphanous, pleated gown and an elaborate headdress. She holds a lotus blossom in one hand and the sign of life in the other. She wears finely crafted sandals. (Tomb at Deir el-Medineh, 13th century B.C.)

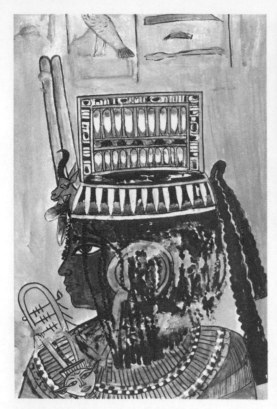

(Above) *An elaborate crown rests on a diadem decorated with lotus leaves. The princess shown here also wears a wig. (Tomb of Menna, Sheikh Abd el-Gurnah, 15th century B.C.)*

A young woman in mourning sprinkles ashes on her head.

On the far right a woman (hand only is seen) spins two spindles of thread simultaneously. The girl facing her passes raw material (probably flax) to be spun. She prepares the material by rolling it along her thigh. Two women weave the thread into cloth on a horizontal loom under the supervision of the older woman standing in the center. (Tomb of Khnumhotep, Beni-hasan, about 19th century B.C.)

gown that went from shoulder to ankles. Often these gowns had long sleeves. Sometimes the right shoulder and right breast were left uncovered. The stark white of the gown against coppery brown skin was sometimes dramatically enhanced by means of a large and multicolored stone-and-gold collar or necklace.

It was only in late New Kingdom times that weaving looms were used to create designs and patterns in cloth used for clothing. Such weaving was used initially for tapestries which hung in homes and tombs. Even after woven patterns were introduced in clothing, white continued to be overwhelmingly the favorite color.

The children usually wore no clothes up until the age of three or four. They also had their hair styled with a child's "topknot." Statues and paintings show children with

43

(Above) *Two maidservants are shown grooming their mistress. Each of the women has a box of perfumed ointment tied on her head. (15th century* B.C.*)*

(Right) *Elaborate collars made of semi-precious stones and gold were stunning when worn with white linen gowns and seen against the coppery brown skin of Egyptian women. (16th century* B.C.*)*

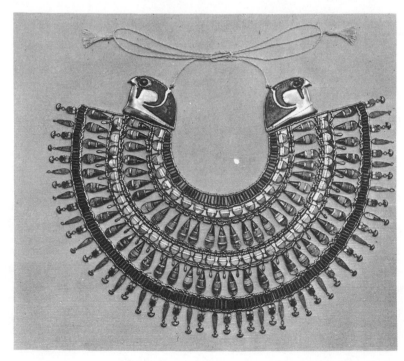

the left half of the head shaved and the remaining long tress of hair braided and draped over the right shoulder.

Sometimes a woman's gown was diaphanous, simply a sheer, flowing covering, with nothing worn underneath it. This was especially true of young budding girls who entertained at parties as musicians or dancers. Young pre-teen or teenaged girls who served as ladies' maids or as entertainers at parties usually went naked in the house, apart from their highly intricate hair style and a gold hip band.

The upper classes, both men and women, wore wigs made from human hair. The women spent much time dying their hair, setting, and arranging it in very elaborate styles.

Egyptian men were usually clean-shaven. The pharaoh was often shown wearing a beard, but that was a kind of "chin-wig" rather than his own beard. It was ceremonial in significance. Even Queen Hatshepsut had herself depicted wearing the pharaonic beard, a symbolic indication of her pharaonic power.

One feature of the Asiatic foreigners that Egyptian artists always showed was their bearded faces. Sometimes the pharaoh is shown holding the decapitated heads of his enemies by their long hair or their beards, thus demonstrating his absolute supremacy over these strange foreigners.

Oils and Cosmetics

Unguents, oils, and cosmetics were vital to the Egyptians' sense of well-being. They prepared scores of varieties of each. To offset the dryness of the climate, these ointments and oils were widely used to preserve the elasticity and softness of the skin. At one time in late New Kingdom times, there was a strike by workers on the royal tombs across the river from Thebes. It was a time of economic hardship. The workers wanted grain rations restored to earlier levels. They also wanted their body-oil allowance restored. Oil was considered as basic as food.

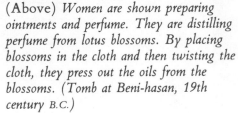

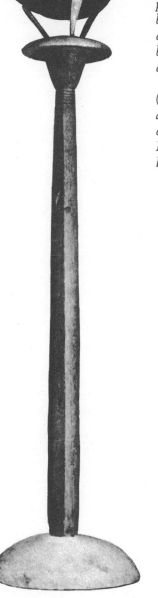

(Above) *Women are shown preparing ointments and perfume. They are distilling perfume from lotus blossoms. By placing blossoms in the cloth and then twisting the cloth, they press out the oils from the blossoms. (Tomb at Beni-hasan, 19th century B.C.)*

(Left) *Oil was used for lighting lamps, as well as for ointments and cooking. The most common oil was pressed from the castor plant. Here is a lampstand shaped in the form of a lotus blossom. (15th century B.C.)*

Eye ointments were used both to enhance the beauty of the eye and to protect the eye against fly-borne eye diseases. Trachoma continues even today to be a major health problem across North Africa and sub-Saharan Africa, spread from person to person by the ever-swarming flies.

Both men and women painted their eyes. A person was often buried with his carved slate palette which he had used for mixing and applying ointments and eye cosmetics. Keeping the very personal palette with the body ensured that the person would have this important and necessary item with him in the blessed Western World of the Dead. The earliest depiction of the pharaoh who first unified the Two Lands, establishing the first dynasty of Egyptian pharaohs, is on a carved slate palette which shows Menes (or Narmur, possibly another name for the same person) subjugating the king of Lower Egypt.

In the home, women had a relatively important and independent role, by comparison with women of other ancient civilizations. At the royal level, inheritance of the throne itself was matrilineal. Some very strong women rose to rule the nation, either as pharaoh or as co-regent. Others, such as Queen Nefertiti or Queen Tiy were obviously very influential in advising and assisting their husbands. Women could serve as priests, as well as temple concubines.

The Great Wife Kawit is shown seated with her maid fanning, her hand holding a cosmetic or perfume jar. The queen smells the fragrance of the lotus while she adorns herself further. (Tomb at Deir el-Bahri, 21st century B.C.)

Paintings show many scenes of domestic harmony. There are thousands of delightful scenes of husband and wife eating together, hunting birds together in the Nile's marshes, fishing together from reed punts, traveling together on the Nile while sniffing lotus blossoms, enjoying music and parties together. Children often accompanied their parents on outings.

A man offers libations to the god Min. His wife stands beside him with her right arm raised in a gesture of adoration. A youth brings a lotus blossom and a dish of spices. The man's wife has a container of perfumed ointment on her head. ("Tomb of the Two Sculptors," Thebes, 16th century B.C.)

(Left) *Women sing as they keep rhythm by clapping their hands. (Tomb of Neferu, 21st century B.C.)*

(Below, left) *A flute player accompanies a singer. (Tomb of Nikauher, Sakkara, about 26th century B.C.)*

They are often shown playing with household pets: a cat, a dog, or a monkey.

Statues of major officials often show the man together with his wife and one or two children. Sometimes, the man and his wife are depicted side by side, standing or sitting, often with her arms affectionately around him. And sometimes the man is shown larger than life, with a diminutive wife and child standing by each of his legs. The wife holds on to his leg tenderly. Whatever the formalized style of statuary, the point is clear that husband and wife honored and enjoyed each other.

Romantic Love and Polygamy

The Egyptians rejoiced in the pleasures of romantic love. Love poems and love songs were a part

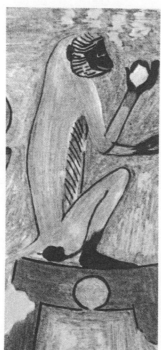

(Above) *The ancient Egyptians loved parties. Here is a dinner party with musicians playing drums and flutes. Some of the musicians are clapping their hands and singing. Nude girls, wearing only an elaborate hairdo and a gold hip band, dance and wait on the guests. The hieroglyphs give the lyrics of the song being sung; it is a hymn to the Nile floods. Note the piles of wine jars ready for use. (Tomb at Thebes, about 15th century B.C.)*

(Left) *Monkeys imported from central Africa were favorite household pets. (Tomb of Rekhmire, Thebes, 15th century B.C.)*

49

of dinner party entertainment. They were either bawdily sung by the diners themselves after drinking plenty of wine or they were charmingly accompanied by the musicians and the nude dancing girls. The songs which have survived are both witty and sensuous.

However honored and loved the First Wife might be, monogamy was not part of the Egyptian family ideal. A man was limited only by his finances as to the number of secondary wives, concubines, and female slaves he might have. Every man of social standing had to have a harem. Nevertheless, the chief wife's legal position was secure, and her children's rights were protected from the claims of half-brothers and half-sisters.

Children in the paintings appear to be happy and carefree. They played

These dancers use sticks in their hands to keep time, while others beat on hand-held timbrels. Note the wigs and diaphanous gowns. (Tomb of Huy, Sakkara, 13th century B.C.)

This woman, baking bread, is raking the ashes out of her oven. (About 25th century B.C.)

Women often worked as professional mourners. Shown here are a variety of stylized mourning gestures: sprinkling ashes or dirt on the head, clapping the hands, baring the breasts, and crying. (Tomb of Thebes, 14th century B.C.)

in the garden and along the river. They learned to use the bird snare, the bow, and the fishline.

Although both boys and girls were loved, every man hoped for at least one son who would inherit his property and see to his burial. Children were married during early adolescence, but remained in the boy's father's home until they reached adulthood.

Especially during the many periods of national peace and general prosperity, Egyptian home life was pleasant and comfortable. It provided opportunity for some degree of individual fulfilment, a luxury not usually available to other ancient peoples.

EGYPT
People at Work

Egyptians were primarily agriculturists. The seasonal fluctuations of the Nile determined each month's activity. The black land of the alluvial deposit required one style of farming; the ground slightly higher than the reaches of the flood, but still easily irrigated through the elaborate canal system, required a different one. There were highly technical terms to describe the different kinds of soils and the different techniques of farming appropriate to each.

Chief among the aids to irrigation was the *shaduf*. This was a long counterweighted pole that was balanced on the top of an upright pole. A bucket was attached to one end, a weight to the other. When the bucket was lowered into the Nile itself or into a major irrigation canal, it could be lifted after it was filled with water with very little effort. The counterweight matched the weight of the water-filled bucket. The *shaduf* could then be easily raised, swung around, and emptied into a field, a garden, a pool, or a higher canal. A single man could readily raise over 500 gallons of water a day by using the *shaduf*.

In the earliest period the soil was turned by using pointed sticks or a short wooden hoe. By Old Kingdom times, a simple plough was developed, drawn by a pair of oxen or donkeys. Seed was generally scattered over the

(Left) *A man reaps his field of wheat with a hand sickle. He holds the top of the stalks and cuts them near the head. A woman gathers the cut grain in her basket. (Tomb of Deir el-Medineh, 13th century* B.C.*)*

(Below, right) *Fishermen used line and hook when fishing the Nile. (Tomb of Khnumhotep, Beni-hasan, 19th century* B.C.*)*

(Left) *The time of harvest shows a wide variety of activity in the fields: two men carry the cut grain to the threshing floor; two girls fight over the gleaning; two men rest under a tree, one asleep, the other drinking his beer. Note the waterskin hanging in the tree and the high stalks left standing after reaping. (Tomb of Menna, Thebes, 15th century* B.C.*)*

Under the supervision of an overseer, farmers prepare land for crops after the annual inundation by the Nile. A hand-hoe prepares the soil where it is still moist; a plough is drawn by oxen where it is drier. Seed is sown broadcast by hand. At the lower left, the food for the field hands is ready for the noon break. (Tomb of Nakht, 15th century B.C.)

field by hand. There were no furrows or rows for planting. Sometimes scattered seed would be trampled into the ground by a herd of sheep or cows which was driven across the field.

Reaping was done at first with a hand sickle. The reaper would hold a bundle of stalks in one hand and cut the tops of the stalks off by using his sickle in his other hand. This required much stooping over, and left tall stubble standing in the field after reaping.

Later the long-handled scythe was developed. This enabled the reaper to use both hands to operate the scythe and to cut the stalks off much closer to the ground.

The grain was trodden out by oxen on hard-packed threshing floors, usually in the open air. Then on windy days, the grain and chaff were thrown into the air. The wind blew the chaff away, which was collected for use as fuel or to bind together mud bricks. The grain fell back to the threshing floor to be gathered for storage.

The grain would be placed in baked mud urns or in larger mud-brick granaries. These in turn would be sealed to try to protect the grain from rodents. Legions of scribes, some working for the estate master and some for the royal bureaucracy, recorded every carefully made measurement of the harvest. The owner, and eventually the pharaoh and his administrators, knew exactly how much grain was stored and where.

Here farmers are piling the harvest of wheat high in the field. The next step is to bale it or put it in baskets and take it by donkey to the threshing floor. (Tomb of Akhhotep, Sakkara, about 23rd century B.C.)

Farm workers are shown in the upper panel beating wheat on the threshing floor with their flails. Standing behind them, a man throws the grain into the air so that the chaff will blow away. A man offers them water from the large water jug to slake their thirst in this hot, dusty task. In the lower panel men collect the grain in buckets. (About 15th century B.C.)

A flax harvester is shown drawing the soaked flax stalks through a carding comb to separate the strands in preparation for spinning. Flax was used for making cloth and ropes. (Tomb of Menna, Aheikh Abd el-Gurnah, 14th century B.C.)

A wide range of fruits and vegetables were grown in every available space. Favorite among the Egyptians were the delicate leeks and onions that flavored most dishes of meat and fish. The poor had an adequate supply of high-protein beans.

Most vegetable oils came from the castor-oil plant and from sesame seeds. The olive was known, but was used for oil only rarely. Oil was used in cooking, for anointing the skin, and for lighting lamps.

The papyrus plant was regularly harvested, although it provided no food. It yielded baskets, mats, boats, twine and ropes, sandals, and paper.

Livestock

Cattle, sheep, and goats were domesticated. Lower Egypt was the main cattle grazing area, due to the constant abundance of grasses. Sheep and goats were herded over the drier hills of Upper Egypt and just beyond the Delta in Lower Egypt. If cattle constituted the herds of the wealthy, goats were the mainstay of the poor. Every home had two or three goats tethered nearby. They could survive on far less food than cattle and still give milk as well as meat.

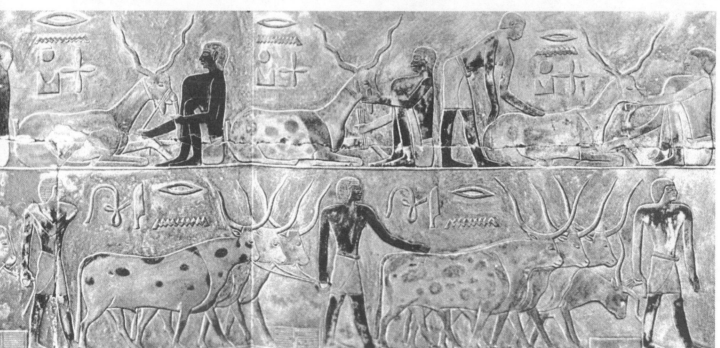

(Top) Herders cared for their flocks outside the fertile alluvial areas in the Nile Valley or the Delta. In the upper left a herdsman carries his own water with him as he drives his flock of goats. He also carries a food pouch and a flute to entertain himself. In the upper right his wife packs his food pouch with round loaves of bread. The lower panel shows the herder in the field with his flock. (Tomb of Api, Thebes, 14th century B.C.) (Bottom) Farm workers fatten stock by hand and then lead the stock to be butchered. (Tomb of Mereruka, Sakkara, about 23rd century B.C.)

The donkey was ancient Egypt's principle beast of burden. (Tomb of Reemkuy, Sakkara, about 26th century B.C.)

The "chiefs of herdsmen" are seen here displaying the best of their herds for inspection. In their hands they hold complete inventories of their herds recorded on scrolls. (Tomb of Khaemhet, Sheikh Abd el-Gurnah, 14th century B.C.)

Herdsmen cared for flocks of sheep and goats in the desert areas beyond the Delta or the Nile Valley. Here a goatherder rests in the shade of a tree, with his staff beside him, and drinks from a jug. A goat at the base of the tree is giving birth, while the goatherder's dog watches. (Tomb of Akhotep, Sakkara, about 26th century B.C.)

Donkeys were raised in great abundance for use in the fields and as beasts of burden. Horses were first raised in large numbers when the Hyksos ruled Egypt. Horses were used to pull chariots rather than for riding. It seems they were also used to pull ploughs or carts.

Specialized Crafts

Besides engaging in agriculture, Egyptians entered into a wide variety of specialized crafts. Some became furniture makers, using either domestic or imported wood. The best furniture was made from Lebanese cedar brought by sea from Byblos, Tyre, or Sidon. The beds were low four-legged platforms with crisscrossed papyrus twine serving as the mattress. Instead of pillows, Egyptians used neck rests that raised the head about six inches.

Chairs were low off the ground.

59

Smiths and metalworkers created gold ornaments with gold mined in Nubia. The six men with tubes are heating the molten gold as part of the refining process. In the middle panel there are samples of the goldsmiths' skills. (Sakkara, 23rd century B.C.)

After horizontal looms were introduced from Asia, fine tapestries were made with exquisite designs. Favorite motifs included lotus and papyrus flowers. (Tomb of Pharaoh Thutmose IV, 15th century B.C.)

The legs on the more expensive ones resembled the front and back legs of lions. The seats were made from papyrus twine, similar to present-day caning. Highly elaborate inlays of wood, ivory, precious stones, and gold decorated the finer pieces of furniture.

Finely made, decorated boxes were fashioned for storing items ranging from cosmetics to clothes and jewelry. More items of fine furniture from the ancient past were found in the tomb of Tutankhamun than in any other ancient site anywhere. These pieces demonstrate the very high level of craftmanship in furniture making at that time.

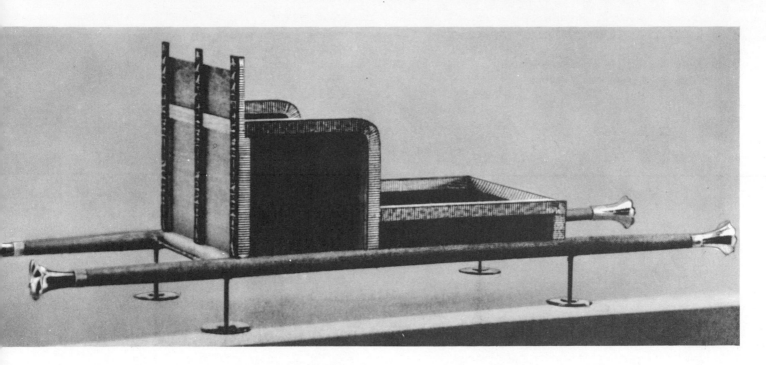

(Above) *Fine furniture making was an Egyptian specialty. This litter was made of wood with gold inlays. It was made for Queen Hetepheres, mother of Pharaoh Khufu (or Cheops). An inscription on the litter lists the queen's titles. (Giza, 28th century B.C.)*

(Below) *Among the products of skilled woodworkers were statues of the sphinx and ebony vessels. Wooden carvings were painted. (Tomb at Thebes, 14th century B.C.)*

Workmen are shown butchering a cow. If this animal had been offered as a sacrifice to one of the gods, the tender forelegs would be given to the priests as their share of the sacrifice. The person offering the sacrifice would eat the remainder of the animal.

Cloth was made mostly of flax. Weavers used a horizontal loom, staked into the ground at one end, and worked by sitting on the ground and holding the other end with their feet while weaving with their hands. This simple loom was used to weave one-color linen cloth.

By New Kingdom times, vertical standing looms were introduced from Asia. Weavers sat before the looms on stools so low that their knees pressed tightly against their chests, often making breathing difficult. These looms were used for weaving both tapestries and designed clothing. Patterns based on the flowers of the lotus and the papyrus were popular with the wealthy.

Some guilds of woodworkers specialized in carving temple statuary and memorial figures. Carvings of the gods, of royal personages, or of important people reached a high level of execution. Sometimes there were several carved statues of the same person placed in his tomb, showing him at several stages of his life from robust youth to lined, stooped old age. In addition, thousands of carved models of people and household articles were placed in tombs. It was thought that the human models would magically come to life in the afterworld, thus providing the master with family and friends, and a full contingent of servants.

Scribes had an important elite profession. They kept records of crops, people, events, knowledge, rituals, and projects. Here some scribes are shown with their pens in their right hands and their case and scrolls in their left. (About 15th century B.C.)

Apothecaries are shown mixing ointments and medicines for healing. They pound herbs with a pestle and mortar, mix them in vats of heated oil, shape the cooled mixture into balls, and mix wines and spices. (Tomb at Thebes, 15th century B.C.)

Workmen rebuild the workshops of the god Amun at Karnak. The pool in the upper left provides water for making mud bricks in forms, which are left in the sun to dry. In the bottom panel, the workmen are using new bricks in the construction of ramps and stairways. (Tomb of Rekhmire, Thebes, 15th century B.C.)

This potter turns his wheel with one hand and shapes the clay into a bowl with his other hand. (About 26th century B.C.)

Shipbuilding was a highly specialized craft. The Nile was Egypt's great highway and her main source of protein—from fish. The Mediterranean provided her with many goods from overseas. Boats ranged from saucer-like papyrus river punts to ocean going vessels that plied the Aegean waters and the southern shores of Africa. Most numerous were the river craft which ceaselessly went up and down the Nile from the Delta to the Second Cataract. These boats used square sails attached to a single mast when going upstream. The steady wind from the north steadily pushed them south. The boats were fitted with oars partly to give them weight when returning downstream with the current.

Most trade was under the pharaoh's direct management, so a merchant class did not evolve in ancient Egypt. The bureaucracy handled trade domestically, as well as internationally.

Trade Links

In the first centuries, the most important trade links went southward through Nubia to the heart of black Africa. Spices and resins for ointments, ivory, skins, and precious stones came by caravan to strongly fortified trading posts in Nubia. There was a complex of twelve forts at the

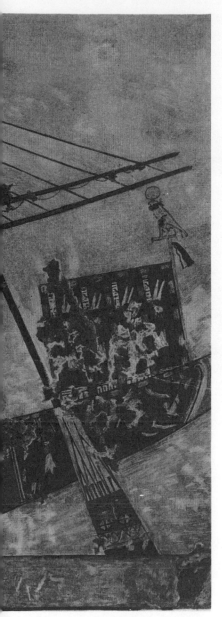

(Above) *The Egyptians demanded fair balances in trade. This drawing is from an ancient papyrus.*

(Left) *Building of larger, luxurious ships required great skill and expert seamanship. (Tomb of Rekhmire, Thebes, 15th century B.C.)*

Second Cataract which protected these vital trade routes. The trading center of Elephantine at the First Cataract got its name because of the vast number of elephant tusks which came into Egypt through that point of entry.

In exchange for these goods from Africa, Egypt provided knives, finished ointments, linens, and grain. Money, in the form of coins, was seldom used for payment. Payment was in goods or in rings of gold. Each ring was of standard weight and purity. Its value varied, depending on supply and demand, much as the gold market works at the present time.

There were several famous over-

seas expeditions to the southern coast of Africa. These trading ventures went to Punt, most probably on the coast of present-day Somalia. The best-recorded of these journeys was undertaken during the reign of Queen Hatshepsut. The Egyptians were especially fascinated by the baboons which were brought back from that expedition.

Tomb paintings show Asiatics of all sorts bringing "tribute" of every kind to the pharaoh. But it is likely that the pharaoh sent back "gifts" in appreciation for tribute. This practice is evidence of vigorous trade activity even though the pharaoh chose to describe it as tribute bearing.

Foreign envoys brought rich gifts and tribute to the pharaoh. He alone in Egypt engaged in overseas trade. Although Egyptian records list these gifts as tribute, the pharaoh often gave gifts in return to show appreciation for loyalty. In practice such exchanges, by whatever name they were called, paid for the trade of goods. Here Canaanite envoys present their tribute. (Tomb of Sebekhetep, Thebes, 15th century B.C.)

Slaves made up part of the work force. This ship is bringing back slaves from Asia. They were acquired either by capture or purchase. These slaves are probably Semites from Canaan. Their hands are raised in submission to Pharaoh Sahure, a 5th Dynasty ruler. (About 27th century B.C.)

Much evidence of Cretan and Minoan goods has been found in Eygpt, indicating that the trade routes went north to the Aegean Sea. Perhaps there was trade with Greece in New Kingdom times. Centuries later, Alexandria was probably the most cosmopolitan commercial center in the entire known world. The Ptolemies built the largest, most impressive lighthouse known to the ancient world to guide ships into the harbor of Alexandria.

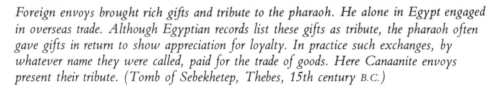

Ropemakers work at the edge of the river, twining multi-strand ropes. Completed coils of rope are seen at the top of the painting. (Tomb at Thebes, 15th century B.C.)

67

EGYPT
A Nation at War

(Left) *When kings were defeated in battle, their bodies were often ceremonially hewed into pieces as a symbol of their complete defeat. This axe-blade of Ahmose (who helped defeat the Hyksos rulers in a war of liberation) shows him in a stylized pose overpowering his foe. Ahmose is hewing his enemy into pieces to demonstrate his overwhelming victory. The blade is designed to hack through mail armor and a metal helmet. The axe is made of bronze and inlaid with gold. (16th century B.C.)*

(Above) *Here the Egyptian chariot corps is shown advancing into battle. Most of the young charioteers were sons of noblemen and provided their own horses and chariots. (Palace of Ramses II, Thebes, 13th century* B.C.*)*

(Above, right) *One man carries weapons common in ancient Egypt: a bow, arrows in a quiver, spear, and a throwing stick (similar to the boomerang). The case protects the bow when it is not in use. (Tomb of Kenamon, Thebes, 15th century* B.C.*)*

The pharaoh was the national war leader, as well as Egypt's ruler and incarnate god. In foreign wars, he usually commanded the Eygptian troops in battle. When the battle was described on memorial walls and burial stones, the pharaoh ensured that his own personal prowess and courage were emphasized. The most flagrant example of pharaonic self-publicity was Ramses II's account of the battle of Kadesh against the Hittites. To read the official Egyptian account recorded on a Ramessid wall is to learn that Ramses II completely destroyed his enemies at Kadesh and that he thereby struck fear into the heart of all nations. But to read the Hittite account of the same battle in the Hittite archives is to learn that Ramses II fled from the battlefield. His terrified troops broke in panic after having been caught in a Hittite ambush. The pull back of Egyptian troops from further confrontation

69

with the Hittites tends to confirm the Hittite side of the story.

In early days of the Old Kingdom there was no standing army on regular duty. If a campaign was to be launched against the Libyans to punish them for excursions into Egyptian territory, for instance, a limited draft would bring the needed troops together. After the completion of the campaign, the army would be disbanded. The civilian-soldier returned to his farm and his trade. A very small royal guard remained on permanent duty, together with a few senior officers around whom an army could be built.

A Permanent Military Force

In time, a trained permanent military force came into being. Soldiering became a regular profession. By the Middle Kingdom, the military were highly regarded. Generals were important and influential court figures. Civilian peasants were trained during three-month low-river times as a kind of national militia, and were proud to be called to duty. (The situation was similar to that in present-day Switzerland, with its tiny regular army and broad-based militia.) In the evenings, older farmers would sit on the doorsteps in the villages by the river, watching the setting sun and the quiet flow of the Nile, as they told war stories of the days of their youth. They wre often buried with their arms besides them in their simple graves, for they wanted to serve the pharaoh in the Western World as they had served him in this life.

By Middle Kingdom times, Nubian troops were hired as mercenaries. If it is surprising that the once feared Nubians now served in the Egyptian army, one need only recall the large numbers of Irish troops that served in the armies of imperial Britain. The Nubians were especially fine bowmen. Egyptian soldiers normally carried spears and shields; the Nubians, bows and reed arrows.

The Hyksos introduced the wheeled car chariot and the war-horse

continued on pg. 88

This mural shows the distribution of rations to the army troops. In the bottom panel an officer oversees the entry of troops for rations into the storehouse. In the middle panel soldiers pick up packs that have already been filled with rations. In the top panel elderly men, possibly retired officers, are waited on and given delicacies. (Tomb of Horemheb, 14th century B.C.)

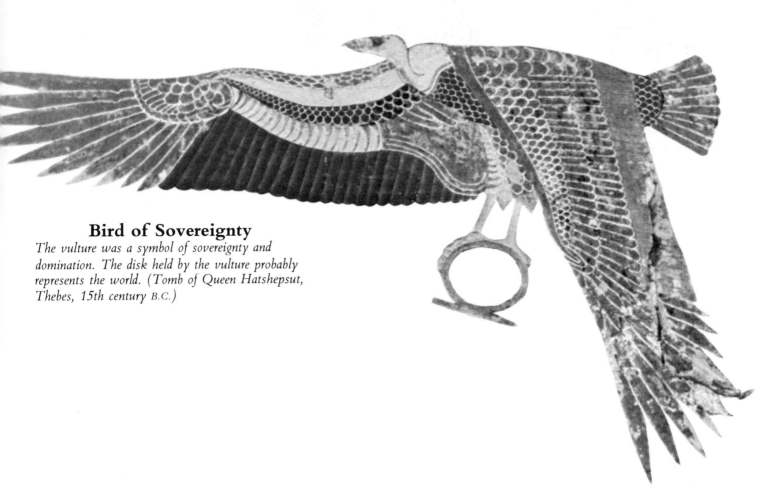

Bird of Sovereignty

The vulture was a symbol of sovereignty and domination. The disk held by the vulture probably represents the world. (Tomb of Queen Hatshepsut, Thebes, 15th century B.C.)

Sacrificial Offerings

Men and women are shown bringing sacrifices. The women carry ducks in their right hands. (Models from tomb of Meketre, Thebes, 21st century B.C.)

Royal Guardian
*Here Senmut, the trusty vizier of Queen
Hatshepsut (Eighteenth Dynasty, 15th century
B.C.), is seen performing his duties as the
guardian of the heiress apparent to the throne.*

Farming

*Models of farmers plowing with teams of oxen.
One farmer prods the oxen on with a long stick
or ox-goad. (About 19th century B.C.)*

Egyptian Revelry

*Two pairs of women dance at a party, while
other women sing and keep time by clapping.
(Tomb of Anefoker, about 19th century B.C.)*

Bringing Offerings

Row upon row of servants are seen in this
relief, bringing to the temple a rich assortment of
produce, animals, and birds as an offering.
(From the temple of Queen Hatshepsut, Deir
el-Bahri.)

Kitchen Scene

*People at work in the kitchen of a large house: a
steer is being slaughtered, in the center beer is being
made, and on the left a woman is grinding wheat
(22nd century B.C.)*

Royal Bodyguard

This soldier is one of the elite personal bodyguards of Ramses III. He carries the typically Egyptian "sickle-sword," a bow, and a quiver of arrows. (Medinet Habu, 12th century B.C.)

Warrior's Chariot

The Hyksos introduced a heavy, four-spoke chariot into Egypt. Princes in Upper Egypt adapted the chariot to Egyptian conditions, making it a lighter, six-spoke vehicle. With excellent tactical development, they used this chariot to drive the Hyksos out of Egypt in the 17th century B.C. The chariot forces were the elite striking force of the pharaoh's army. (15th century B.C.)

Hippo

The hippopotamus lived in large numbers in the Nile. Because it ate crops that grew along the water's edge, farmers hunted the hippopotamus. This faience model is decorated with drawings of the lotus blossom, a favorite food for the hippopotamus. (Middle Kingdom, 1990-1780 B.C.)

Cobra

The cobra was an often-used symbol of royalty in ancient Egypt. The crowns of the pharaoh and his "great wife" were often decorated with a cobra, indicating their status as divine rulers. This statue of a cobra is made of gold and was found in the tomb of Tutankhamon. (15th century B.C.)

Grape Harvesting

Vines grew in abundance in the Delta area and at the great El Faiyum development. Here two men are harvesting grapes for wine making. (Tomb at Thebes, about 1500 B.C.)

Crocodile Amulet

An amulet in the shape of a crocodile, a feared man-eating river dweller. This amulet was probably placed in a tomb to protect the owner from any crocodiles he might meet in the afterlife. (Ptolemaic dynasty, about 50 B.C.)

Farm Steward's House

In this model of the house of a farm steward, a woman kneads dough to make bread on the ground floor. The steward sits in the sun on the roof. (About 20th century B.C.)

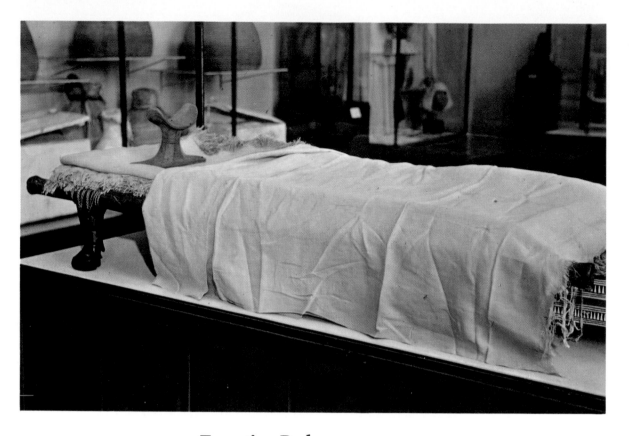

Egyptian Bed

This bed is from New Kingdom times. Note the linen covering, the headrest, and the reed "mattress and springs." (About 15th century B.C.)

Bronze Mirror

A mirror made of polished bronze was a valuable possession. This one has the name of the owner engraved in the handle. The wooden handle is overlaid with gold. (Tomb of Renseneb, Thebes, 18th century B.C.)

Scribe

Imhotep was a scribe, architect, medical scholar, and administrator renowned of the Old Kingdom. Here is a statue of an Old Kingdom scribe ready to write. (Sakkara, about 25th century B.C.)

Marsh Birds

Birds of all kinds were found nesting and feeding in the Nile's reed marshes. Bird snaring was a favorite sport, and provided delicate dishes for eating. (Tomb of Kenamon, 15th century B.C.)

Egyptian Servant

*An Egyptian servant in a wealthy home carries a basket of
fruit on her head and a duck in her hand. (Tomb of Meketre,
Thebes, 21st century B.C.)*

Nebethet

A finely executed statue of the goddess Nebethet, sister of Isis. (6th century B.C.)

Ramses II

(Left) *A statue of Ramses II. The coiled serpent in the center of his crown is a symbol of the pharaoh's sovereignty. Ramses II built great temples in his own honor at Karnak and Abu Simbel. this statue is believed to have come from the Karnak temple. (13th century B.C.)*

(Left) Egyptian soldiers carried a shield and spear. Nubian bowmen augmented Egyptian troops. (Tomb of Mesehti, Asjut, about 22nd century B.C.) Above is a wooden model of an Egyptian shield. (19th century B.C.)

A barber combs and sets the hair of a recruit to the pharaoh's army. He sets it with grease from the bowl at his feet. (Tomb of Userhet, 15th century B.C.)

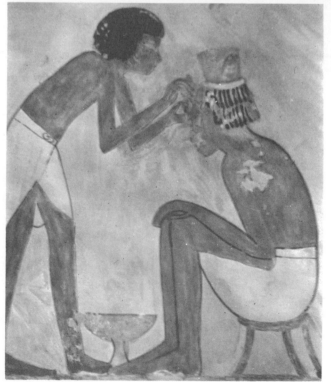

A stylized portrait of a pharaoh shows him smiting his foes. The slate palette of Menes (Narmur?) who first united the Two Lands shows the victor in this pose. Here Ramses III is shown wielding an Egyptian curved sword with one hand, while he holds his conquered foes by the hair with the other hand. (12th century B.C.)

continued from pg. 70

during the Second Intermediate Period. The Hyksos chariot was a heavy four-spoke affair. After some experimentation, the Egyptians in Upper Egypt adapted the chariot to the desert conditions of Egypt, making it a lighter, faster, more mobile six-spoked chariot. They also developed effective battlefield tactics. Then they turned this weapon system (horse, chariot, driver, bowman, shield-bearer) against the Hyksos themselves. With the improved chariot, the Egyptians drove the Hyksos from Egypt in the war of liberation. The Egyptian cavalry force, composed of chariot teams, was the dominant weapon in winning the empire of the New Kingdom.

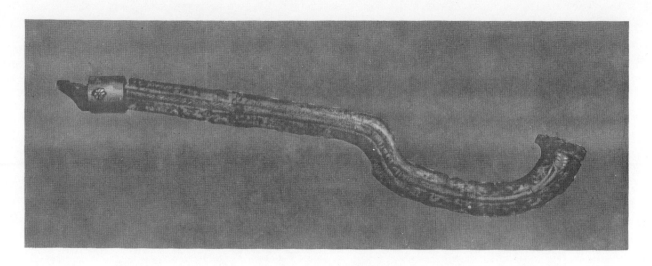

(Above) *The Egyptian "sickle sword" provided a longer edge for slashing (the outside edge of the arc) than would a straight sword. Early swords were made of bronze and easily lost their sharp edge in battle.*

(Below) *Captives taken in battle were often brought to Egypt as hostages or as slaves. Here prisoners of war from Canaan are led at the end of a rope. The facial features and hair styles of some in the lower panel indicate that they are Hittites. (Tomb of Horemheb, Thebes, 14th century B.C.)*

The chariot force considered itself the elite branch of the army. It was made up mostly of young aristocrats who provided their own chariots and horses.

The Military Class

As the imperial New Kingdom grew to maturity, the military became a well-established class. Soldiers traveled abroad, drew garrison duty overseas in Asia or in Nubia and Kush, became wealthy through taking booty, acquired slaves and foreign women as part of the spoils of wars, and received generous veterans' benefits in the form of food and land back in Egypt.

The regular Egyptian army was augmented by elite groups of foreigners. There were corps of black Nubians, Palestinians, Syrians, Libyans, and "Sea People" (possibly Minoans forced south by Greek expansion in the Aegean).

Eventually, the army became so powerful that it could name one of its generals as the new pharaoh. Such was the case shortly after the death of young Tutankhamun. Horemheb was commander-in-chief of the army. To head off political anarchy during the struggle for the succession, he administered the nation for a time. At the appropriate moment, he marched at the head of an army into Thebes and had himself proclaimed pharaoh, the first of the Nineteenth Dynasty. Not surprisingly, Horemheb was a believer in strong central government.

Ships were used primarily to provide transport and supplies for the army. When the Sea People began to invade Egypt during the time of the Ramessid period, Egypt developed fighting ships. One of the most dramatic battles recorded on Egyptian walls was won at sea by Ramses III when the Sea People were decisively repulsed.

A census of every family in Egypt was recorded by royal scribes. Location of the home, names of the family, and occupations of all family members were carefully compiled. When a call-up for additional troops was issued, the names of individual men from these royal census records

Here a pharaoh is shown with his implements of war. (12th century B.C.)

were selected to serve. Troops were drawn evenly from every district of the nation. Young men were no more willing to serve then than they are now in unpopular wars, so police were often required to ensure that the selectee was actually inducted into the army. The police were also used to track down draft evaders or deserters.

90

Horemheb was a general who took over as pharaoh and founded the Nineteenth Dynasty. Here Egyptian courtiers are shown rendering homage to Horemheb as is due to the new ruler. (14th century B.C.)

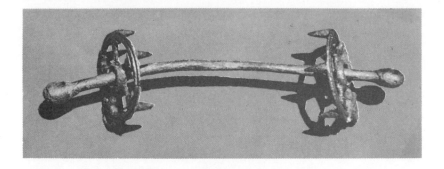

A bit for controlling horses from the Hyksos period is shown here. The Asiatic Hyksos rulers introduced the horse and the war chariot to Egypt. (Tell el-Ajjul, about 18th century B.C.)

The Egyptian sword was shaped somewhat like a sickle, except its cutting edge on the outside of the blade. This made it more like the later scimitar with maximum cutting edge used for slashing rather than thrusting. (Gezer, 14th century B.C.)

This is the handle of a dagger which belonged to a high official. It is made of an alloy of gold and silver with an embossed hunting scene. (Sakkara, 18th century B.C.)

EGYPT
The God-King

The key to Egyptian stability and order over a 3,000 year period was the unique regard in which the pharaoh was held. He was seen to be king, god, the father and mother of all the people, the shepherd of the nation, the owner of all things, high priest, chief justice, military commander-in-chief, and head administrator. A more absolute monarchy cannot be imagined. Even the Nile itself flooded because the pharaoh willed it!

In theory, not often in practice, the pharaoh owned all the land. Therefore, all the foodstuffs grown on that land were his. In years of excess production, the surplus was carefully accounted for by royal scribes and was sent to storage in royal storehouses. In years of crop failure due to low flood levels, locusts, or blight, the pharaoh, as father of all the people, fed them from his storehouses.

As the god-king, the pharaoh owned the minerals of Nubia and the trade routes to Asia. No one seriously challenged his rights to these royal monopolies. They made him enormously wealthy and enable him to negotiate from great strength with foreign rulers who did not have similar resources immediately at their disposal.

The pharaoh served as head of all the priesthoods. He generously provided land, grain, and gold for them. But he was far more than a high priest. He was god incarnate, sometimes several gods. Sometimes he was the son

The pharaoh ruled an empire divided into four main sections: Mizraim (Egypt), Kush (Nubia and Kush to the south), Phut (Libya to the west), and Canaan to the east. Representatives of peoples from those four sections of the empire are shown here. Egyptians were shown as red-skinned; Nubians, black; Libyans, white; and Canaanites, dark brown. (Tomb of Seti, 14th century B.C.)

Horus, the god of Memphis, in the shape of a falcon, spreads his wings above the head of Pharaoh Chephren, affirming the pharaoh's divinity. The pharaoh and Horus are one in ruling the land. (Giza, 27th century B.C.)

The Pharaoh Amenhotep II is shown sitting on the lap of his nurse, indicating support and nurture. His enemies, Nubians and Semites, are shown on their knees under his feet. Their hands are bound behind their backs, and the Pharaoh holds ropes which are tied to their necks, indicating complete submission. Above the Pharaoh's head is the sacred goose of the god Amun, sheltering the pharaoh in the shadow of its wings. This entire picture shows the privileged position of the pharaoh as the god-king of Egypt. (Tomb of Kenamon, Thebes, 15th century B.C.)

of two gods. The names of the gods and the seat of their power changed from time to time as the dynasties changed, but the pharaoh was always an incarnate deity.

Each city had its own local god. If a city rose to national power, the god of that city became the god of the pharaoh. Thus it became the chief god of the nation during that period. What is more, the pharaoh was that god in the flesh and ruled with that god's power.

Horus, Re, Amun, and Aton are some of the major gods identified with pharaohs down the centuries. Even Cleopatra, at the end of the pharaonic line, was understood by the people to be Isis incarnate. When she committed suicide in Anthony's tomb, she was dressed as Isis.

When the peasants were summoned on a three-month work draft before the Nile's flooding to labor on royal projects, they served their god-king willingly. This was especially true in the earlier dynasties, before the times of disillusionment which set in during the First Intermediate Period.

The greatest honor an Egyptian could have was to serve his pharaoh well, and to be recognized in some way by the pharaoh in return. Sometimes the pharaoh gave a noble a title which told of the confidence the pharaoh placed in him. Sometimes a finely wrought gold collar was given to the noble to be worn on official occasions. Every person so honored was sure to tell about it at great length on the walls of his tomb.

During the imperial expansion of the New Kingdom, the administrative tasks of the pharaoh increased many-fold as the size of the empire grew and as foreign relations grew more complex. He had to be in full command of his army on a day-by-day basis. His army was one of the largest military forces of the time numbering more than 20,000 troops.

It is impossible to separate the strands of motivation which led the pharaohs to construct the vast temple complexes along the Nile. There was certainly the element of religious duty—the pharaohs being both incarnate gods to the people they ruled and

Syrians bring tribute and gifts to the pharaoh. One brings his small daughter as a hostage to be raised in the pharaoh's household and possibly married to one of Egypt's royal princes. (Tomb of Sebekhetep, Thebes, 15th century B.C.)

representatives of their people to the gods. There was also the desire on the part of the pharaoh to qualify for purity in this life and to win happy continuance in the Western World of the Dead. Surely too, there was the desire to outstrip all earlier pharaohs by building on a larger, more luxurious, more grandiose scale than they. The ceremonial aspects of both religion and state were united in the person of the pharaoh and were immortalized in the buildings he caused to be erected.

Lines of Royal Succession

The throne passed to the next generation through the eldest daughter. Except in very rare circumstances, this woman did not rule in her own name. However, marriage to her

(Left) *Taxes were paid in kind, since coins were not used in ancient Egypt. Here officers of districts in Upper Egypt are seen bringing their taxes in the form of agricultural produce, cattle, goats, and rings made of gold and silver. (Tomb of Rekhmire, Thebes, 15th century B.C.)*

(Below) *The pharaoh was often depicted as larger than life, for he was seen as the god-king and far more important than mere mortals who might appear in the picture with him. Here the pharaoh leads a hunt into the desert, a favorite sport for the rulers. (Tomb of Tutankhamun, 15th century B.C.)*

conveyed the right to be pharaoh. She was then designated the Great Wife. Her eldest daughter was the following generation's Great Wife.

Egypt's political struggles took place far from the public eye. They centered around the question of which prince would marry the heiress, and, by so doing, secure the throne. The pharaoh had a large harem, with many gradations of wives and concubines. Sometimes there could be as many as seventy or eighty sons of the pharaoh who could claim some right to the throne. It was usual for the heiress to marry one of these half-brothers. It was theoretically best for her to marry a full brother, if there was one, thus maintaining the purest possible royal bloodline.

If the Great Wife had no daughter, the heiress could be designated from princesses of royal blood. Once she even came from outside the royal family—when Amenhotep III raised a commoner, Tiy, to that exalted position.

During the later New Kingdom, the priests played an increasingly influential role in choosing which prince would marry the heiress and thus become pharaoh. The priests claimed special magical powers that enabled them to read the mind of the god Amun in choosing which prince should become Amun incarnate.

Often the chosen prince was made a co-regent during the latter years of his father's lifetime. The two would then rule jointly, the son being subservient to the father. Thus, Thutmose III co-ruled for about twenty years with his aunt, Queen Hatshepsut, before he ruled alone in his own right after she died. The experience must have grated on his spirit, for he tried to obliterate her name from every temple and monument she ever raised.

This complex system of determining the royal succession worked well for ancient Egypt. Altogether there were thirty-three dynasties of pharaohs during a 3,000-year period. Yet there was seldom civil revolt. The transition of power was usually peaceful. The bureaucracy readily transferred its loyalty to the new god-king. For the

The Dowager Mother of the pharaoh sometimes served as co-regent with him. In any event, she was always highly honored. Here Amenhotep I is seen seated with his mother, Queen Nefertari. ("Tomb of the Two Sculptors," 16th century B.C.)

(Right) A daughter of Ramses III is shown in a procession on her way to offer a sacrifice. The princess is seen in the upper left, wearing a high headdress. She and her attendants carry staves with lotus blossoms as offerings to the god. (Temple wall, Medinet-Habu, 12th century B.C.)

The pharaoh bestowed honors publicly on those he favored. Here Horemheb is shown being appointed as one of the pharaoh's generals. He has just had a gold chain placed around his neck and his daughters are embracing him in delight. More royal gifts are being brought to him. He himself later became a pharaoh of Egypt. (Tomb of Horemheb, 14th century B.C.)

people, life went on without noticeable change under his protection.

A Concept of Justice

In administering the government, the pharaoh was guided by the ideal of *ma'at*, the primary Egyptian concept of justice, which was a combination of order, truth, and justice. This principle was embodied in the person of the pharaoh: he was guided by *ma'at*, and what he decided became *ma'at*. His duty to the principle of *ma'at* and to the people was to see that his administrators and his courts of law were ruled in accordance with this principle. It was not codified into written law. One found out what *ma'at* was in any specific situation by seeking how a pharaoh, living or dead, had judged a similar case. *Ma'at* was something like common law, embodied in the decisions of generations of pharaohs. It allowed new kinds of cases to be dealt with as the nation developed, but at the same time it was essentially conservative; it was rooted in the will of pharaohs past.

Courts took testimonies. Penalties for perjury were harsh, for that was seen as an affront to the pharaoh himself. Court records were strictly kept by an army of court scribes. In criminal cases especially, testimony was often taken with the accompaniment of severe police beating, or the threat of police beating, as an accepted part of the interrogation process.

Some offenses warranted the death penalty. Among them were treason and perjury. In some very serious cases, burial might be forbidden, thus denying a person his afterlife. Sometimes punishment would be mutilation of some part of the body or consignment to forced labor in the mines of Nubia. The most common punishment for minor offenses was beating.

The policing of Egypt in New Kingdom times was assigned to the Medjay, a select body of Nubian gendarmerie. They were similar in function to the Guardia Civil in modern Spain, a national semi-military police force with

(Above) *The pharaoh ensured that crops were measured accurately. He was then able to determine the ratio of taxes in kind to be levied. In this painting royal tax officials are overseeing the measurement of the crop before harvest.*

(Top, right) *Beating was the most common punishment in ancient Egypt. Here a village head who tried to evade taxes is being beaten by tax officials. (Tomb of Mereruka, Sakkara, about 23rd century B.C.)*

offices in every town but responsible directly to the national chief of police. Like the Guardia Civil, the Medjay also provided security patrols on the borders.

There was a large contingent of courtiers and attendants who ran the royal household. Their duties ranged from food preparation to the education of royal children; from management of the royal harem to expertise in international protocol.

Court life was highly ceremonial. The pharaoh spent much of his time in ceremonial duties that were part-religious, part-diplomatic, and part-governmental. The stronger pharaohs were able to control their bureaucracies and to assert themselves beyond the time-consuming demands of protocol so as to set their own stamp on Egyptian life. The weaker pharaohs were guided by their administrators and wholly occupied in their ceremonial and administrative obligations, yet the life of the nation went on as before without skipping a beat.

The pharaoh was usually shown wearing the intricate double crown of the Two Lands. He held a crook, representing his role as shepherd of the people. He also held a scourge or lash, representing his duty to enforce *ma'at* throughout the land. He was sometimes shown overshadowed by his god. The god might be represented as a sheltered falcon (Horus) or a crowning sundisk (Amun or Aton). The symbol of the god and the figure of the pharaoh, joined inseparably together, eloquently testified to Egypt's good fortune in being ruled by a god-king.

EGYPT
The Cult of The Dead

(Above, right) *A part of the* Book of the Dead *is shown. In this book the soul of the deceased person is guided in reciting all the sins that he has not committed; this proves his innocence when seeking admission to the Western World of the Dead.*

The ancient Egyptians were noted in their own times as being the most religious of peoples. For modern man, who tends to understand religion, at least in part, in terms of its logical consistency, the religion of ancient Egypt may seem incomprehensible. The ancients saw no need for such consistency. Gods moved from city to city for reasons not clearly known. Myths and legends about the gods changed from generation to generation with tenuous connections between the stories. The Egyptians loved to speculate about their gods and their effect on this life and the next. This endless speculation was recorded in detail on the walls of tombs and in papyrus scrolls used in magical incantations. But this great amount of speculation led to constantly evolving and developing theologies which cannot be succinctly unraveled.

The fact that the gods were shrouded in mystery helped support thousands of priests, whose task was to stand between the people and the gods. Unlike many of the gods of other ancient civilizations, the Egyptian gods were essentially beneficent rather than

A physician, wearing a leopard skin as a badge of his office, sprinkles perfumed ointment on a man and his wife.

(Left) This picture shows bags of embalming materials, which were usually placed with the mummy. These were taken from the tomb of Tutankhamun. (15th century B.C.)

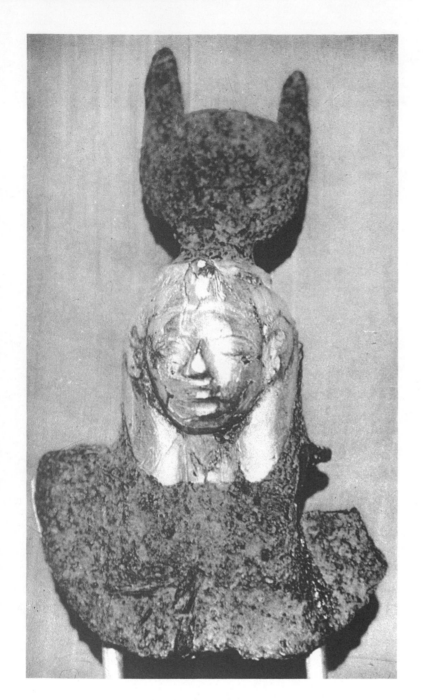

Tarharka was one of the pharaohs of the Nubian dynasty who attempted to restore the glories of the classical past. Here Tarharka is seen presenting an offering to Horus, the god of Upper Egypt, often represented as a falcon. (9th century B.C.)

This is a bronze head of the goddess Hathor. It is overlaid with gold and probably fit on the end of a military standard. It was discovered at Beth-Shan in Canaan. (About 14th century B.C.)

malign. The people loved their gods, with all their attendant ceremonies and mystery.

Local Gods

Each city, town, and village had its own god. The people of these locations sought the local god's blessing down through the centuries, regardless of which gods might dominate the national life at any particular time. This local god was often known only by the name of the place itself. The god of Edfu, for instance, was known only as "He of Edfu." Ptah was the god of Memphis; Sekhmet was the goddess of Memphis; Amun was the god of Thebes.

These local gods usually had no powers beyond the geographic bounds of their locality. However, as the influence of a city grew, so did the influence of that city's gods. Horus, for instance, became the god of the whole of Upper Egypt in predynastic times because Horus was the god of the city which became the capital of Upper Egypt. When the Two Lands were unified, the pharaoh Menes, who was the king of Upper Egypt, moved his capital north to the new city of

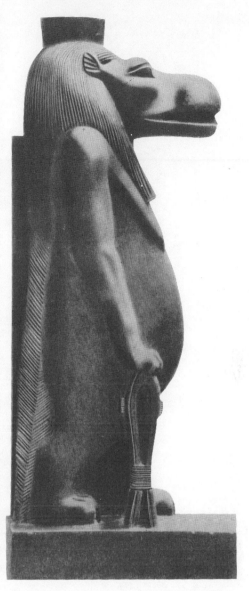

The demon Bes, wearing a crown of feathers and surrounded by monkeys and geese. Figures of Bes have been found in many graves of common people, for he was a favorite among them.

This picture is of the goddess Taweret. She is shaped like a large woman with the head of a hippopotamus and a wig with headdress. Her feet and hands are lion's paws. (Karnak, 7th century B.C.)

This picture shows a man kneeling and doing obeisance under a heavily laden palm tree alongside a water canal. The hieroglyphs are from the Book of the Dead. (Tomb at Deir el-Medineh, about 13th century B.C.)

A pharaoh offers unguents to his god. This stele was erected by the pharaoh in commemoration of good fortune in his life.

A pharaoh protected by the god Horus. Horus is shown in semi-human form with the wings of a falcon. He shelters the pharaoh under the shadow of his wings. The pharaoh wears the crown of Upper Egypt.

Egyptians who served the pharaoh were given titles of importance, and commemorated this honor in their own tombs. Neferyu was given the title "chancellor" or "sole companion" of the pharaoh. He tells about it on this funerary stele and shows a picture of himself sitting in the palace at the top; he and his wife are seen on either side of the palace door at the bottom. (Tomb of Neferyu, about 22nd century B.C.)

Here is a sensitively rendered statue of a woman with uplifted gaze making an offering to a god. (Gebal, about 15th century B.C.)

Memphis. He also moved his patron god, Horus, to that location. Horus was then the chief of the gods of Egypt, and the pharaoh was Horus incarnate.

The same pattern was repeated as the dynasties changed, as new pharaohs rose to power under the patronage of other gods. The name of the patron god was often incorporated into the name of the pharaoh, as in Amenhotep (Amun), Ramses (Ra or Re), or Akhnaton (Aton).

Sometimes people moved to establish a new city elsewhere in the country. They would take their local gods with them. The god would now have two places, quite far from each other, where he was honored. Sometimes a particular god would appeal to people who belonged to a special craft or profession. Montu of Thebes became a wargod, honored by the army. Hathor, a goddess of Dendera, became a goddess of love and joy, honored throughout the land. Ptah of Memphis became the god of metalworkers and smiths.

There was a great number of lesser gods, demons, and spirits who could bless or harm people. Their blessing was sought or their wrath placated by constant use of magical formulas and actions. Even in America today many people hesitate to walk under a ladder for fear of stirring up some spirit of ill fortune. Life for the ancient Egyptians was governed by such rules and practices, well understood by everyone.

Protective household deities were honored in the form of Bes. This grotesque figure has been found in many ordinary graves of the common people. Ugly as he may appear to modern eyes, Bes was a beneficent god.

Gods visited one another, intermarried, had children, moved, and changed their form. They were often represented by pictures or statues of a human male or female form with the head of the animal which was traditionally associated with that god. For example, Hathor had the body of a woman and the head of a cow; Horus had the body of a man and the head of a falcon. Sometimes Horus would be

A man named Ram, who was a doorkeeper, suffered with a crippling disease such as poliomyelitis. Here he is shown bringing an offering to the Canaanite goddes of healing, Ishtar, and is accompanied by his wife and child. (A stele found at Memphis, 14-16th century, B.C.)

seen as a falcon hovering above the pharaoh's head.

There were constant religious festivals honoring the gods. At many of these celebrations the presence of the pharaoh and his court was required. The royal barges took the pharaoh and his party up and down the Nile, providing the villagers along the river with a chance to see the pharaoh in his splendor and to join vicariously in the festivities.

Preparing for the Afterlife

The Egyptians cared deeply for their dead. The first responsibility to a dead person was the preservation of the body, a means of assisting the person in entering the afterlife. The mummified body itself, stone or wooden statues of the person, and pictures of the person painted or carved on the walls of the tomb were all useful in ensuring that the person's spirit had a body to inhabit upon entering the other world.

A guild of embalmers chanted elaborate embalming formulas over certain parts of the body as they worked. The methods of embalming became highly stylized and filled with religious meaning. The brain and viscera were removed and placed in four special jars, called Canopic jars, which were guarded by special gods. Every action and every wrapping had its own secret name and history. The emalmers put on the dog-faced mask of the cult-god Anubis during certain times of their work on each body.

The mummy was often placed in a series of coffins and sarcophagi. Magical formulas were painted or carved on the coffins to enable the dead person who convince the gods, who weighed his heart for signs of wrongdoing, that he was innocent and should be ushered peacefully into the Western World of the Dead.

Death was seen as an unwelcome intrusion on the orderly cycles of life. Successful passage to the afterlife resulted in the restoration of the person to the happy, unchanging cycles of the universe.

This picture shows part of the Valley of the Kings on the western bank of the Nile across the river from Thebes. So far, more than sixty royal tombs have been discovered in this area.

110

A model of herdsmen driving a herd of cattle in front of the estate owner for his inspection. Seated near the owner is a group of scribes who record the size and condition of the herd. This record was used partly for tax purposes and partly for farm management.

Death interrupted the cycles of life. The Egyptians cared deeply for their dead and engaged in elaborate ceremonies at great expense to help the dead rise to happiness in the afterlife. Here is a stele showing public mourning. In the front is a shrine, then members of the family of the deceased, then professional mourners. One of the mourners stoops down for dirt to sprinkle on her head. (Abydos, about 6th century B.C.)

Farmers bring grain from the fields (top panel) to be stored in the estate granaries (middle panel). The grape harvest is completed and men tread on the grapes in a large vat to make wine (bottom panel). The men hold onto a horizontal pole to keep their balance.

Importance of the Tomb

The tomb was the owner's base to his afterlife. The owner lived in the tomb or visited it from the other world, following a rite called "The Opening of the Mouth." At that point the statues and paintings in the tomb were somehow vivified. The owner was given food, servants, chattels, friends—all in model or pictorial form—to take with him to the afterlife. The ritual of the Opening of the Mouth turned all these pictorial representations into spiritual realities.

Relatives, friends, and descendants could visit the person in his tomb. There was even a visiting chamber with a peephole for viewing a

This picture shows a funerary meal being served to a dead man. His young son stands before him with a lotus blossom in his hand. (Tomb of Sarenput, 21st century B.C.)

statue of the person. On special feast days, people came to family tombs to share a meal with their deceased ancestors.

The dead lived in a happy place, sometimes called the Western World, where the sun went during the night. Sometimes the abode of the dead was called the realm of Osiris, the god of resurrection.

Safe passage to the afterlife was based in part on having lived a good life, one characterized by fidelity *to ma'at*. Many of the incantations used to convince the guardians of the after-life that the person was true to *ma'at* are preserved in the *Book of the Dead*.

The paintings and carvings in the tombs of ancient Egyptians show a love of life and a joy in nature that enchants viewers thousands of years

Egyptians cared deeply for their dead. Here a mother weeps at a funeral. (Tomb at Sakkara, 13th century B.C.)

later. The original purpose of these artistic representations was to grant immortality to the deceased. And indeed through them, the ancient Egyptians live for us today as do no other people of antiquity. Five thousand years later we marvel at their vitality and splendor.

EGYPT
Recurring Patterns

The birth of civilization occurred in a region bounded on the east by the Indus River, on the north by the Danube River, and on the south by the Sahara Desert. Egypt during the New Kingdom was the dominant world power. For centuries, she remained a major power as other nations crossed the stage of history.

In time the center of the world shifted west to Rome, and then eventually to northern Europe. For centuries Egypt lay forgotten in the sands, ruled by unknown caliphs and pashas. She was only an African adjunct of the Ottoman Empire, far removed from the flow of world events.

French and British conflicts over the passage to India in the nineteenth century brought Egypt back into world focus. Napoleon occupied the Nile in 1798. He brought with him an army of scholars as well as an army of soldiers. They marveled at the splendors of ancient Egypt, recovered and catalogued them, and shared their discoveries with the world.

Early in the second half of the nineteenth century, a Franco-Egyptian company built the Suez Canal. In 1875 the British bought a controlling interest in this company. In 1882 the British occupied Egypt in order to control this vital waterway, the link with their Asian empire.

Even though Egypt became technically independent in 1922, the British forced a treaty on the Egyptian government which permitted British military control of the canal zone for twenty years. Before that period ended, World War II broke out. Egypt served as a major British base throughout the war.

The Changed Character of the Middle East

The character of the Middle East changed radically after World War II. The state of Israel was established. The British and French left their Arab protectorates; and they now became independent Arab nations: Syria, Jordan, Iraq, Egypt, and Lebanon. The British also left Iran. Middle Eastern oil became a major factor in world economics and in Great Power rivalry.

The area also became an arena of an East-West Great Power conflict between Russia and the United States. When Egypt failed to secure funding for the Aswan Dam from the United States, she turned to Russia for assistance for a time. Russia was only too pleased to establish her presence along the Nile.

The United States had close links with Israel, but at the same time desperately needed Arab oil. The Arabs and the Israelis were unable to agree on peace settlements of any sort and several inconclusive wars erupted over the three decades following the establishment of Israel. Both Russia and the United States worked to keep Middle Eastern conflicts from escalating into a Great Power war.

By the last quarter of the twentieth century, the Middle East was a major locus of international conflict. The heated issues were awesome: the question of the legitimacy of a Jewish homeland and of a Palestinian homeland; the politico-religious struggles between Christian, Jew, and Moslem; the control of the world's major oil reserves and the power exercised by nations controlling those reserves; the imminent dangers of the possible use of nuclear weapons.

Present Concerns Reflect Pharaonic Concerns

These issues placed Egypt back into world awareness. Her 1977 peace concerns and policies are contemporary reflections of concerns and policies that the pharaohs addressed. Indeed, they are rooted in Egypt's geography and in her centuries-old traditions.

Ancient Egypt was a land of five to ten million people who lived on the rich bounty of the Nile River. Water management was crucial to national survival.

Because of the discovery of the modern wonder drug, penicillin, and its widespread use during World War II, Egypt's population today is three to four times the size of that of ancient Egypt. Control of the Nile for optimum food production remains the main business of Egypt's government. Construction of the High Dam at Aswan is modern Egypt's answer to her desperate need for an increase in year-round agricultural production to feed her people. When she sought help for this primary internal need, Egypt and the dam were swept up in Great Power conflict. The Egyptian government had no choice. She had to develop the Nile's resources or else lose the confidence of her own people.

Her relations with neighbors are complex. Egypt and Libya have had a love-hate relationship for centuries. Some of the fiercest raids against pharaonic Egypt came from the western desert. If the Egyptian was the settled agriculturalist, the Libyan was the rough marauding warrior. Sometimes the countries were linked in alliance; sometimes one ruled the other. Most often they lived in uneasy antagonism.

In modern times, Egypt's relations with Libya have fluctuated between federation and undeclared war.

Egypt's southern borders were once her most important. She annexed Nubia, and Nubians became an integral part of Egyptian life. Today the waters of Lake Nasser cover most of Upper Nubia. Egyptian technicians assist the modern Sudanese in every kind of developmental project. Arabic-speaking Sudan is still a close ally and economic partner of the populous nation to the north.

On the eastern frontier, ancient Egypt always preferred to have client states east of the Sinai Desert to protect her eastern approaches. Present-day Israeli occupation of the Sinai Desert places hostile forces far too close to the Suez Canal and to Egypt's main population centers for her liking.

Although ancient Egypt was the most populous state in the Middle East, she was never able to control, for any long period of time, the city states of Syria, Lebanon, and Palestine. These city states always struggled between themselves, dissipating their chances of becoming major centers of power. Such is still the case today. In terms of population Egypt is by far the largest Arab nation. In recent years, she has several times tried unsuccessfully to link herself with Syria. Egypt must still deal with each state in the region on a piecemeal basis. Thus Egypt's current unilateral dealings with Israel are nothing new.

Ancient Egypt was the most religious of nations. For centuries Cairo was a center of great Islamic learning and devotion. The religious variety of present-day Egypt includes conservative Islam, ancient Christianity, modern Islam searching for its way in today's world, and a growing secularism.

Although present-day Egypt is linked with her Islamic neighbors both financially and historically, she will not be bound to them. She maintains her independence as a proud nation, conscious of her glorious heritage. She is committed to national growth with dignity and magnanimity, as befits the descendant of the pharaohs.